# Mowgli's Almanac
# CHEWED
# BY FIRE

**A Hitchhiker's Account**

# ISAAC POTTENGER

ISBN: 978-1-7350308-0-7 (Print)
ISBN: 978-1-7350308-1-4 (E-book)

20 21 22 23 24     10 9 8 7 6 5 4 3 2 1

Interior Formatting & Cover Design by Rachael Ritchey

# TABLE OF CONTENTS & DATES

Introduction...........................................................................................i
Chapter 1 ............................................................................................1
   8.11.07......................................................................................1

Chapter 2............................................................................................5
Chapter 3..........................................................................................10
Chapter 4..........................................................................................13
Chapter 5..........................................................................................17
Chapter 6..........................................................................................21
Chapter 7..........................................................................................23
Chapter 8..........................................................................................26
Chapter 9..........................................................................................27
   3.3.07........................................................................................27

Chapter 10.........................................................................................31
Chapter 11.........................................................................................33
Chapter 12.........................................................................................38
Chapter 13.........................................................................................40
Chapter 14.........................................................................................42
Chapter 15.........................................................................................46
Chapter 16.........................................................................................48
Chapter 17.........................................................................................51
Chapter 18.........................................................................................54
Chapter 19.........................................................................................57
Chapter 20.........................................................................................60
Chapter 21.........................................................................................63
   9.6.1988 ...................................................................................63

Chapter 22.........................................................................................66
   8.25.07......................................................................................66

Chapter 23.........................................................................................69
   5.22.08......................................................................................69

Chapter 24.........................................................................................71
Chapter 25.........................................................................................75
Chapter 26.........................................................................................79
   6.9.08........................................................................................79

Chapter 27.........................................................................................82

6.11.08.....................................................................................82

Chapter 28..............................................................................85
Chapter 29..............................................................................90
   6.13.08.....................................................................................90

   6.17.08.....................................................................................92

Chapter 30..............................................................................94
   6.19.08.....................................................................................94

Chapter 31..............................................................................99
   6.24.08.....................................................................................99

Chapter 32............................................................................ 101
Chapter 33............................................................................ 102
   6.29.08................................................................................... 103

Chapter 34............................................................................ 106
Chapter 35............................................................................ 109
Chapter 36............................................................................ 111
   7.5.08..................................................................................... 111

Chapter 37............................................................................ 113
Chapter 38............................................................................ 118
Chapter 39............................................................................ 120
   7.10.08................................................................................... 120

Chapter 40............................................................................ 122
Chapter 41............................................................................ 125
Chapter 42............................................................................ 128
Chapter 43............................................................................ 129
   8.6.08..................................................................................... 129

Chapter 44............................................................................ 131
   8.15.08................................................................................... 131

   12.6.08................................................................................... 132

   12.10.08 ................................................................................. 132

   12.13.08 ................................................................................. 133

   12.15.08 ................................................................................. 133

   1.23.09................................................................................... 134

Chapter 45............................................................................ 136
   6.1.09..................................................................................... 136

Chapter 46.................................................................................. 138
Chapter 47.................................................................................. 141
Chapter 48.................................................................................. 147
Chapter 49.................................................................................. 148
Chapter 50.................................................................................. 152
Chapter 51.................................................................................. 154
Chapter 52.................................................................................. 160
    3.15.12.................................................................................. 160
Chapter 53.................................................................................. 162
Chapter 54.................................................................................. 167
    6.21.13-6.22.13 ·································································· 167
Chapter 55.................................................................................. 171
Chapter 56.................................................................................. 173
Chapter 57.................................................................................. 177
Chapter 58.................................................................................. 179
Chapter 59.................................................................................. 181
Book References ......................................................................... 183
Music References ....................................................................... 186
Movie References ....................................................................... 187
Website References .................................................................... 187
About the Author....................................................................... 188

# Mowgli's Almanac
# CHEWED
# BY FIRE

# *Introduction*

## RIDDLE ME THIS:

### CAN AN OMNIPOTENT GOD CREATE A ROCK SO HEAVY HE CAN'T LIFT IT?

Suddenly, waking naked in thought, it is I, who has become the weaker than the innate survivalist. For it is 'they' who hold the most powerful presence in the thing I fear the most.

Where I live, I do walk alone in the backwoods where the grizzlies and the wild wolves roam. I don't always see, but I do double-dare to sit still in the nadir of a night—not just momentarily, but metaphorically, forever.

Most of us sleep or turn on the electric lamp to curb the distance felt from our beloved sun. We carry a different kind of fire now, but as always, the animal kingdom finds its subsistence and comfort during those darkest of hours.

Verily the spirit is not straight forward: humans have no claws, no winter coat, no three stomachs…To subsist naturally, we don't live because we let live, but, due to our demon-strative behaviors, it begs the question, "Aren't the animals begrudged?" "Aren't the humans depriving the non-human life their rightful place on this earth?" Given our weird power, that answer is definitely, "yes". Humans are observably anthropocentric: self-preservers, pro-*us* life. I view *us* all as rebels without a clue. We act like seasick sailors deranged from the overfamiliarity of the same, stale environment, stumbling into a New World; reborn, revisited into a different form…

Is the reader a person with a sense of destiny?

I put forth the proposition that the animals lucidly dream in yours as they are clearly in mine. I see the demons depicted by exaggerated forms of the tiger. There has never been a faceless evil emerging from out of the night.

All new times and tables teach how the past may become the present; however, never guess what a backwards man-cub might tell you. Entire species on this periodic table of elements have died so that we could breathe from this. When do we return the favor? What more could be said of a poem's struggle? Thrown into this life, a boy can only expect so much when he is given a single moment in time. He looks around with penetrating eyes as if he's never been able to see before, forever gasping at such presence around him. Everything is the owner of perfection and nothing need be changed. It is already so. The crystals within maintained the precious moments but refused to offer any refraction unless he was the one to shine first. It is only then that the relationship seems beyond life. True marriage births the death of all ego, and the struggles forthwith, join together and take chorus in the tavern's tabernacle choir (as if with a life of their own).

By reading this book you are undertaking a journey. When angry or melancholy, I may just jive more harmoniously. If you are happy where you are, then leave me be.

The story and metaphor of Mowgli is my most favorite that I have ever heard. I frequently imagine Mowgli coming out of the jungle and being adopted by a Christian family. He grows up, starts smoking and studying the world's philosophies for a thousand years or so. He soon grows tired of everything but when Mowgli tries to go back to the Jungle, it kicks him back out...That is what happened.

I only succeeded as Mowgli because Mowgli is not Hindi. Rudyard Kipling holds that the name does not come from any tongue, rather, "Mowgli" is from the language of the Forest. Idealistically, I am attempting to exist within and without those un-spoken languages. The tangible writing of this book is from my study, memory, and my "non-descript" journal rewritten. Understand this book as it is: a creative dialogue, written in order to understand our multiple-personality concepts.

# 1

8.11.07

## THE FIRST DAY OF HITCHHIKING

Executioner's feeling for too long.
We've been like possessed Skelos
Without any muscles.
"Where is the flesh on these bones?"
Without constant renewal,
<u>This</u> is not *Home.*
If life you seek,
then death you shall surely meet.

Do not think him too cruel,
Nay he is wise
And could never take *you* before *your* time.
Renew myself! And wake up
to a day devoid of Time.

It had been nearly peaceful winding along the bank of the Snake River outside of Massacre Rocks State Park. I am a sun worshipper, albeit that day, was blistering, with sixty pounds upon my back. Up ahead was the crumbing, basalt embankment, blasted out of a slope to allow room for Highway 86 and its vehicles. I was not excited to scramble over hard, by foot, having been already scrambled. I was close to over-heating, so I decided to make use of an upcoming boat dock. Slowly, I peeled my cotton clothes off like redressing a wound and I dove in…

Away from home, it was the first day of a new journey incoherent to the wristwatchers. It felt like I was on my own time and I wasn't coasting along by the asphalt; rather, I was trudging across the Snake River Valley in the southeastern part of the State of Idaho on foot. I had ventured to walk the one-hundred and twelve miles from just outside of Pocatello, Idaho to the City of Rocks National Reserve.

The morning had been a field of headless stalks of wheat beyond bone dry, so sharpened by the sun they were like razor blades to my bare skin. As I passed by the Pocatello airport, Runway Patrol rolled out to look me over as if I was a twin-towers-terrorist. I admit, I've felt like one, but definitely nothing healing that day. The American Falls reservoir is an ocean inside the midst of a desert. Every sandy banked stream I found opposed my procession like an impassable Nile. I hiked the dune its entire breadth with undrinkable waves lapping the shoreline, kicking sand fleas, and wishing it was at sunset. When I did reach Massacre Rocks State Park, it was a paved path, yet, I preferred it to be otherwise still.

The river has its share of boaters churning up the bottom left and right, and upon docking from my river cleanse, I considered consulting one of her river queens for a ferry. For all the life of me, I did not want to be bottlenecked on or near that highway. I sat for a moment. I didn't have to wait long and a truck pulled up. Out of it came humans naturalizing their animals on the very pier that was my temporary "door-step". They were there for some of the same that I was, as dogs are to water. After we exchanged formalities, I started packing up and making for the road because in my mind, I was in it for the renunciation of the paved way, discomfort or no. They stopped me. "Where are you headed?" they politely inquired, as I was slinking away, acting like there was someplace else to be. The answer to some questions is like a domino without its antigravity, pulling only one course. I fell into their stock F-250 with a smile on my face. There was no way I was going to be upset as a different dream manifested within the greater one. I mean sure, my thumb never left my side, but when a baby first steps you should hear the crowd. It's the way I felt inside. This is just how the hitch-hiking started. The spark that emboldens was still there. I made the condition before getting into their truck that I only desired to go a short distance. I just wanted to get past the narrowing of the path without ignoring how I came to that little present. They would have taken me all the way to the town of Burley and possibly beyond. There was a horse trailer awaiting their pick-up and had I asked them, it was possible I could have been in the City of Rocks that night. I asked them to drop me off one exit before the Raft River Valley rest area. With their sincere farewell and my appreciative wave goodbye, I walked on.

Venturing away from the highway, I hiked up some grassy hills to meet a field, where some Spanish-speaking farm hands were wrapping up their gloves for the day. As they were leaving, I entered. Setting up camp, I pocket-rocket boiled some water for my oatmeal and slipped into my bivouac sack to lay my head down to rest before the day had fully set.

## 2

Soundly rested, I woke up before the sun did the next morning. Cultivating the predawn stretch and shedding of sleep from my eyes, they met the horizon. In one direction there was a distant lightning storm with blue shards of broken glass cracking a wide, black cloud, revealing what really is beneath the veil—more lightning. To my left, the horizon was filled with actualized smoke. Several fires had started burning someone's fields and the sky was being cloaked with black and red after excitement was cast by those cloudiest of gods. The day commenced with the dance of elements erupting simultaneously in full color as the sun crested over the scene.

I crossed a street parallel to the highway making my way to the Rest Area water faucets. I took advantage of that iconic building. I cleaned my pans, filled my pack with water, washed my face, and began trekking diagonally across the entire Raft River Valley desert.

Be it man or beast, barbed-wire is the feral child's bane. Under these circumstances the two are indistinguishable, for the path I am on is between them both. I tracked the deer into badger burrows and collected perfect crow feathers, watched metaphysical cinema through the mind's eye, and longed for wire cutters. I spotlighted coyote as he ducked below the horizon into unseen valleys. That wild dog has always kept me at a distance but always seemed to come up from behind. Some may say, "pull the trigger" "shoot at her" on most sights...Argumentatively, coyote is too prolific. Argumentatively, we are too. I felt I was walking through the sagebrush Garden of Eden, bordered by the fields of entre-manuring humans.

I began to view my horoscope'd experiment as predictable. The landscape became a grinding factory. Hiking through the sage upon hill, upon valley, upon sage hill… Here's a fence where some agitator tried to claim it as his own. Oh, and here's another one, and another. "I'm happy for you and your burdensome quarry . . . even though you both look very thirsty." "It's a divided union when one outlives the other, Romeo!"

In that state of mind with that day in time, I was in need of something different. Only momentarily but not wanting for dramatic effect, the sun took a siesta behind a cloud. My eyes relaxed. Blinking back clarity, what I stepped into was a wild grass land, soft and abounding. There is no question, it was like a woman's whisper, after all the grease was used up and the ear could only hear sounds of a burning clutch, a seemingly untouched beauty like nothing I had experienced before. The even softer wind, honored by the bowing of the grass in waving salutation, cooled those feverish tremens with a patting of a towel.

Walking out into the world away from that naturally occurring pillow of grass was harsh. The rabbit and bitter brush gave off the sensation of being terribly angry with me. A land bridge has its toll to be paid and the ferryman wants your water, be it bloody or no. It's easy to drive a car. It's even easy to ride a horse. I mean 'shit' just wear a pair of jeans and the plants can't say, "shit." I decided beforehand and left those behind. I wore my running shorts. It was then bare skin on bare branch the entire way. The native is eternally disappointed in me because I would not be as they were. I won't ignore. I can't ignore, but I still got my water from the very sprinkler system that resupplied the outpouring of this one's displacement. I would have felt just like those desert plants if I was rooted, thirsty outside a field of foreign crops, watered even in the heat of day.

Up ahead held a thirty-mile stomp and it became ironic—I walked out of water. The 3 liters I was carrying were gone…Back then there were few moments when the body spoke up. At that time, mine said, "If you go any further it's going to be difficult to recover". The sun was setting and I was already feeling needy for want of hydration. On my map, there was a creek bed, and I was making every effort within me to get there on time. I charged across parched land through brush bitter and sage to find nothing more than a drought and a missing piece of my borrowed equipment. The stream bed was there but without any water.

Leaving the stream, I dropped my bag and followed tracks of deer weeks old. They spelled a time I was new to but this place had known. A garter snake slipped and slithered up, up the bank but not away because I caught him. Without my bag, I retraced my steppes. "Where's my knife? Where's my dad's knife? I'm out of water but where's my dad's fucking knife!?" I was almost to the town of Malta but I was going in small circles the opposite direction. Black handle . . . steel blade. To me, my father's pride knife, just gone. As I said, the sun was setting and then it had set. I released the knife to the night but not without a headlamp rescue party attempt. Onto the street, to all those afraid of axe murders and midnight raping, I beseech thee! I carried a full bag with an empty scabbard. Weaponless and thirsty in the middle of the night, I walked the road south to Malta with my thumb reaching out. I knew of a convenience store, (most likely closed, but maybe with a faucet), further down the road. That was still a distant light! As I drearily approached, the answer was just a hoarse whisper but it was still there. sShud sShud sShud sShud Ckshckshckshck-shhhhhh! A tempo drummed by that many thumbed elephant-man, Gannesh, himself, destroyer of obstacles. Someone was watering their grass! I rejoiced fully clothed and kissed that sprinkler. No filter required.

I crossed to the opposite side of the road and spread out in a corner of some vacant lot of grass to eat some food, look up at the sky and close my eyes.

"Sweating stars and straining to learn a new song, having listened to it only once, without practice, another one begins. It's a madness I am refusing to pace without. My belief is that somewhere layered beneath our nervous system that land song is being programmed. Body will someday remind of every note ever heard and all the streams of thought that flow, carry towards one end. With every rest and every action that this soul has urged, by faith, these trials are in that one direction of destiny, not destination. Capacity to meet destiny's end has never been exhausted for it happens most powerfully when everything sleeps."

# 3

After a dry, nine miles deep the next day, the sun had met its zenith and I was getting prodded on by gun-point by the blinding star of the local sheriff. Like a bandit, I walked on or be forced to relinquish my water to the high noon. Something was getting cooked and smelling crispy. It wasn't bacon. It was just my brain. I wasn't eating very much and the sixty pounds weighed approximately six hundred and fifty with the constant flow of water weight. When I actually found a flowing stream, I almost overlooked it. But by taking double, I knew better. A nearby congregation of cattle forced me to the other side of the fence where the grass was greener, and after watering on some higher grounds, I napped beneath a lonely shade.

"Yep, mmhm. Gotta drink upstream from the herds."

Nomadic animals are forever bound to the temperament of the sky, and Heaven's personality loves to dance between its bipolar extremes. Not even a day since I was so fatigued for want of it, the clouds, filled with lament, gathered together and released, a deluge. The first wave was manageable. The wailing ended shortly, choked down as if startled and looking around, but when an emotion is interrupted it is bound to come up again. I put on new socks thinking it was over. I never wanted to wear cotton again. In my bag, the sweaty clam was both damp and stinky making their home as much like them as possible. When I looked up the second time, I saw it wasn't my emotional ruling. This time it was a total fallout aimed right at me. Trees and a poncho can only offer shelter under tears of joy. I got so waterlogged I looked pathetic, yet learning can happen quickly. Especially for under which circumstances someone can proposition a questing driver. No one likes a wet dog. A wet mongrel is even less welcome. Lo and behold, my right thumb lost its potential to ignite a rescue fire. I didn't have time for dejection with squish squish after every step, squish squish, getting me closer to my destination.

I was taking the metronome real slow after that. Relax or burn out. The storm had passed with plenty of day left and the sun was at about two o'clock with three the horizon. Even though I was sweating a river, my clothes began to dry out. I had left my yard stick at home, but I knew that the one-hundred and twelve miles had shrunk drastically. I had aced the junction, north to Burley, and had gotten through beyond Elba. Something within me reassured me that my distance was there. With the hip straps from my backpack, drawing blood from abrasion and the blisters on my feet, though taped up, were constantly growing, I truly started to feel like, I had passed some weird kind of test.

I was out of the pressure cooker and the sunlit mountains smiled, showing benevolent approval, allowing their radiance to precede every experience I had ever known. It was at that pristine moment, I looked around and raised my thumb. The next person to pass by, pulled over.

.

# 4

The ride was a god-send yet the driver proved indifferent. The man driving was stolid beyond eye contact right from the beginning. I had thrown my bag in the back of his beat-up, old Chevy and then He told me where the drop-off point was. Nothing else was said the entire duration of the ride.

Unlike the clean, congenial, and soft waver of the previous machine, this one had worked beyond its intention. Some stones never smooth as time wears on them. Instead, their edges are accentuated and if handled wrong, cut. The humane richness of the air I breathed said to me, "You are not going to understand who I am, so why bother making pointless noises". Those silent cried, "MY way has gone too long without recognition. Who cares for yours?" I noticed his dinner of homegrown corn and other vegetables. That's all a man needs, isn't it? The complexion he carried made me unsure. I couldn't even smile comfortably. By this seeming alienation of me, it appeared that this was a man hardened in-complete routine. He let me out within the city limits of Almo. Hastily avoiding any thanks, he pulled his truck around and was gone.

The manner sobered me. I watered myself at the only gas station around, and kicked off in cooled spirits with a couple miles left to go before sunset. Literally walk to the end of the line, because straight ahead is where the pavement ends. Dirt turns into fields eventually becoming Utah, so choose the right (CTR). Welcome to the City of the Rocks!

"I don't see anything."

Juniper trees sprout their hold upon Smokey Mountain rising higher than its neighbors to mask the City of the Rocks Reserve from out-of-sight. Its smoky haze is the curtain between. Walking past the pastures on the left and the right side of the road, I hid away beneath some of those scraggy, saggy, Jupiter limbs for the night's nest. With my head boughed, the sun would rise with me on that hike into the valley of the sacred granite kings.

The City of Rocks National Reserve is a rock climbers' dream space. It was the way I was introduced to this place: Idaho State University's Outdoor Program. By chance, I went on one of their field trips. It was the first time I was strung up at the top of a rock formation called Bread Loaves. With my belayer yelling at me to climb over the edge backwards, "Hold on to the rope, not the rock…Trust the rope." From there, my mind was blasted with a shot of adrenaline as I got stuck on a ledge and had to leap of faith backwards to get over it. A fleeting weightlessness, and an out-of-body lurch—the rope held. Needless to say, I wasn't

completely enamored with the sport of jumping from ledges
. . . but I wished to be.

If you, the reader, is not familiar with the City of Rocks
National Reserve, most likely one is with Walt Disney's
"The Lion King." Bring the image of Pride Rock coupled
with the first sight of the elephant graveyard into the same
view. Strewn about are fossilized granite skeletons far too
massive to be from any deceased mammoth's frame. These
bleached paleoliths are on par with our imaginative
impressions of the dinosaurs. "I can do anything," but this
is the Queen's bottom jaw of that which humbled those
terrible lizard kings. Like hyenas, life keeps peeking through
their empty sockets and making insane cackling in the
middle of the night. The pride in any of these rocks could
either lift me up in a lover's embrace or drain the vitality
right out of my hands. They can churn the sky like a
cauldron, conjuring 90 mile an hour wind tunnels, mounted
by lightning bolts and/or hailstorms. No exaggeration.

If the community supporting the pride had
disapproved, Rafiki would have dropped the newborn cub
over the cliff.

By a natural blue sky in the cool slant of the early
morning, I was wearily welcomed. Despite tracking my
omens the entire way, I was feeling agitated…and becoming
more so. My body was there but there wasn't that sense of
satisfaction I was looking for. It took a network to move
any distance on this planet of paradox, but I felt myself still
in a desert. I couldn't trust any map, after I renounced the
manmade pumps. I didn't know where the streams were in
the heated climax of the boiling Fall!

Two weeks prior, I had been there before by means as
driven with friends. In stepping-stone fashion, we moved

from rock to rock solely through the portal of a combustive machine, but when I left this place last, I went away starving. I thought the hunger pangs were an evidence of a void, a voiceless vacuum refusing all other life its life procession. The mind had become curious about a feeling and there blossomed only one choice or let it all die. I had to come back. I had to water that seed of curiosity. Not by my thoughts of freewill but by my agreement with what would be required to catch up. My adventure required different means to get to this very place at this exact moment or forever sever the taste for it. I put everything I had into just getting there.

When you find yourself at the crossroads: left, right, or wait? The most prodigious choices are that simple. I could only pick one. Life has its ways and has always demanded more than that, but not while I'm on a walkabout. Coming from the east entrance for the first time on foot, rather than left, I went right, towards the lookout point. I must say, this cub's naivety will always prevail looking for that one perfect "spot." It's not supposed to be found rationally. Still, I was trying to, and in the search for water, I fell headfirst off the precipice into the lemming's vast ocean.

# 5

## MUSICIAN—MUSE-MAGICIAN

It seems to rain a lot, but nothing ever sticks. "Shrug" No spots. At that time of that year, the only flowing water in the entire City of Rocks was followed beneath the shadow of her granite canine, Stripe Rock. Her sharp tooth has been scarred by the formidable strike of a quartzite lightning bolt, hence the stripe. It became the holy symbol for water. Only one day older…

## "I know why she swallowed the fly."

A little flirt, her clothes were short
then out in the world unprepared
She let out a scream!
As to not miss a beat
They fought for the best seat
They knew she could snort
But didn't know she could sing
Her screams turned to tears
Salty snacks better than they've had in years
All one-hundred and sixty-five
Single file just didn't jive.
She ducked and clucked
They sucked and mucked
Some tickled her toes others played tag on her nose
It wouldn't have ended there . . .
That's why I know why she swallowed the fly.
Not just the one
but the whole troupe of 'em
One thousand tiny pegs
Across her exposed legs
Drove her to the brink of where?
I can't even think . . .

Sitting in a heated moment being driven mad by all the cow's flies, I jumped up and burst from the cloud into a clearing and yelled from the bottom of my lungs to any that might hear, "WHY DID YOU BRING ME HERE!?" It was from somewhere deep within my mind that replied clearly through my body, "Take it."

I had planned to take mushrooms after I arrived…but I had unknowingly carried with me the remains of Thailand's acid. Unknowingly crazy, yet completely schizophrenic in the 21st Century, I consented and tasted of a metallic tinge, to the tongue as an *ergot* poisoning to dispel the Dark Ages. Forever more, becoming a hunter in the rye.

---

This was the first time I met her. Maybe from fantasy or my take on the creative influence, a sort of external identity manifested into my vision. I saw the liquid blue ooze into my mind from an archetype of what to me is Female. She flooded my mind. I didn't want it. In fact, I was split in two about the entire engagement. It was so close to bodily possession, I have to call it that. I spent a year painting the picture I started that night. I called her my Lady Electric on canvas. I play myself like I am Virgo and the experience was something liberating in-kind unknown.

---

Having just taken acid in the City of Rocks, I hiked East from Stripe Rock and climbed the bleached fins of a stegosaur rock; long gone, but still here. Atop, where the sun beamed bright and the voices were clear, the sun colored through my eyes closed into kaleidoscope visions. A peace washed out and over me at the sight of incomprehensible patterns. From out of the sun, she came as the woman dressed in red, and every shade thereof; taking face in her own aspects of nature every time I see her. She was once blue coming out of the music. I've seen her smiling green from the grass. I have heard no fell voice to steal from the soul. Instead, she is in likeness to something untamed yet ethereal, ancient and calm. All the while, there are kindnesses of creativity so that one might be filled with more than they once were: Aphrodite, Infinite Priestess, Pachamama or just some great dreaming woman.

Separate from and as innocently as I could, I made an instrument of the goliath vertebrae. Peaking my head into the pockets of erosion, sounding like a didgeridoo, the tones of my vocal chord, harmonized with the ghost notes that had gotten long petrified in those rocks.

I summoned the insects, and the sky grew territorial. The weather changed. Standing up and looking out across the white and grey rock-scape, the clouds started to grow menacing and the birds desperately flapped to the strobe light acidity of the cool-aid in my eye. My heart free, willed joy only shown from a parent's attention. The wind tested my footing and the lightning struck between distant rocks on the horizon. The rain and sleet whipped my bare skin, but my eyes insisted that I was recognized! Shockingly, the electricity demanded the same in return and we threw our tantrums together. There were no vultures soaring above my drumming heart chambers. My dream-wolves were howling and at bay. I was gifted a hailstorm that possessed a signature of a surreal reality we all live in. Where I found myself was where I was.

# 6

It was a short-lived storm; ending as suddenly as it began. And after the land smelted down to the doldrums, the wasps, the ants, the grasshoppers and the flies all resurfaced. Each carried their own personality as diverse as something without orientation to dimensions: upside down and around, omni-directional minds. I put on my poncho and went naked to and fro as an overseer of the dynamic plays of every carapace covered creature I could find. In amongst the sagebrush and lupine, I watched a desperate struggle of ants against an army of sturdier ones. They dodged and reeled with timing through a staggered march of bigger ants. From stone to pebble, they waited and bolted like a rabbit from tuft to patch between a stream of dangerous coyotes. They felt so conscious. I was the referee to the grasshoppers leaping up and announcing their territories with sustained flights that competed by hovering and clicking in the air to see which bull could stay up suspended longer than his rival at every elbow in the dirt trails weaving through the rose and dumpy-eared flowers. I have never witnessed consistency.

# 7

The following morning, the landscape tantalized for that ceremonious freeclimb up the petrified Buddha's like an irregular nudist. I wore my climbing shoes and chalk bag but I didn't know what it would feel like to be liberated until my fears quit hiding who I really am: politically on the edge and scared of falling. The weather posed no threat with the sun winking at me behind intermittent clouds, as if saying, "Come on, up you go." It's not necessarily concerning this human being to being. It's between the mirror and a naked animal. I scouted a line to minimize some of the deadfall exposure. I coated my hands in magnesium carbonate to absorb my already sweaty palms like a puffball mushroom releasing spores. I approached and started climbing. Hands then feet, foot, hand, then feet. I felt like an unnatural lizard with tunnel vision. Electric confidence wears off and the climb had a spook to it. But I made it. Naked as a noonday loon under a midday crescent moon, shaking like an adrenal junkie, I perched as a marmot at the top of some approximate-foot tall formation.

## "The bright-Side of the Web"

There is something there
In the trees. In the light coming through them.
The grass, the fallen limbs, and crumbs of stone.
It shows that the earth was crawled upon in the night,
From glandular liquid to fibrous solid
Catching a breeze
To glide effortlessly along
It does not fall short of the glory of
One can see it creasing the scene
In their own shimmering strands of silver
Like an organic wrinkle on the still life ocular.
Imposing an en-lightened geometry,
Furtive design,
The difference of a day and of a night.
What is revealed and what is still hidden
The centered, centripetal
Fifth directional

Come now, come down. No one is with the guarantee that their motion is free from stumble upon the wells of sorrow. My emotions empty in order to be filled by a deeper well and sprigs of fresher springs, but pouring out watery tears to parched places is an amazing experience of itself. To do this, many times, it means timing the foot into places when parched of humans.

I don't sit too long for the optimization of the latent potential in a person. That sense of suppressed, rather than exploring nature wreaks havoc on the view of the wildness in ourselves. We need catharsis. The call of the wild is strong in all hearts, and I know mine can only beat half-heartedly until answered. If we were still sent out from the village, in the mandatory-spirit quest modality, I don't believe this estranged society would have ever been allowed.

We have become the hypocrites of conflicting desires unless we learn how to devolve and walk alone . . . to find that we aren't. I had no "buddy" there to comfort me, so I found friends from different casts. I ceased to feel alone like the dog can make you feel. My multiple-personality is trapped between the tragedy and the comedy with convenience as my motto. If you aren't crazy, I don't know what's wrong with you. As if waiting for something to swallow them up, newer communities lack the ability to renew themselves and tend to share in some prideful understanding as equally as in an ignorance.

The planet would flourish just fine without human presence, but if these "pests" were eliminated, the entire totem would crash down in unceremonious death. Because these creatures carry more than their own weight, I thank the ants and the flies for their songs in my side.

*8*

The fourth day since my arrival, I exodus from the City of Rocks to just beyond the city of Almo before I thumbed down a fellow climber from Colorado: Captain America. I bought him a sandwich, and that hitch brought me in a single shot all the way back to my township of Pocatello. I walked there to get this baby to walk. It was my own toddling task but it is the task for those living with luck without reason. It is the task for those hunting with luck for reason. It's a seeking breathe. The exhale is much longer than the inhale. An amphibious bull-shit-frog might croak one last time over its dualistic dominion but the kingdom of water will always take on another form and slither forward across the land. My own relationship with mystery would take me by the hand in that feminine aire and tell me, "Everything is going to be alright."

*9*

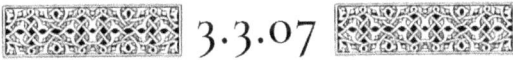

SOUTH OF THE 44TH DEGREE KRÄBI,
THAILAND

"no-Side to the inter-Web"
Thesis, Antithesis, and Anthesis
I don't know . . . yet
Hypothesis, Experiment, and Time Taken

Emerging out of an auto-pilot's fog, I stepped into the Taipei International Airport. Going through any airport with baggage checks and lines that connect, I feel as if I step onto a conveyor belt that has little signs reading, "Keep arms and elbows inside the ride at all times."

A single-serving friend had given me a valium to help with the sling-shot-space-ship shuttle across the Pacific, and unsure if I even wanted it, it went into my pocket. Taiwan was just a layover. The deal breaker was if we could get all the way into Southern Thailand. Bangkok is in the south central, and we had one more flight even further south along the peninsula, before Kräbi.

While standing in line with our luggage going through the scanners, the people ahead of me were getting the shakedown. Remembering the valium, I quietly panicked without a prescription and stealthily swallowed it.

It was probably a good time to take it anyways. My travel companion had put up with me losing my passport, then my ticket, then my passport again. The entire time they were just in a different pocket. I lost reason on the way to the other side of the world with way too many pockets. I was nervous, but I wouldn't have admitted to it. The uniformed scanner guards kind of intimidated me, and they could quickly become the antagonist to . . . well . . . anything. I had just graduated early from high school to spend a month in Thailand-climbing rocks. For me, it was the first unguided passage flight out of the parental nest. There *is* a high mortality rate at this stage. The confusion of climbing gear and snorkel fins, coupled with books and clothes was helpful but it wasn't what I was depending on. Within my copy of Tom Wolfe's *Electric Kool-Aid Acid Test,* I had taped up a pouch of tin foil containing the tabs. There were enough to share but not to sell, and I had no intention to distribute as a pusher. I took those tabs of acid with me by trusting a piece of mind that was just awaiting a personal illumination. A climbing friend told me once, "When in doubt, dyno out!" "Go big or go home". I'm saying "Go big by your own measure or, I guess, never do."

---

*Sawasdee krahp!* That sense of release crossing customs into Thailand was truly something blurring. To and fro, our eyes tried to take in too many things at once only to find an odd attraction to the door to the outside. We weren't alone, but we were still, our own welcome committee. Taiwan's airport had felt constricting but the international one in Bangkok was expansive. Their ceiling was an arena worthy of a Roman era, multicultural exchange. We bartered down an upfront taxi driver, and loaded our things into his trunk to change airports for the domestic flight south.

The taxi man eye-balled at us through his rear-view mirror as if he had something to say the entire ride. Maybe he was just guessing where we were coming from? I don't know. Pocatello, Idaho. The language barrier *is* something worth building a tower of Babel to get across. Then again, domestic dreams are easily forgotten.

I had lain my head back on that rickety flight south without ever remembering closing my eyes. The plane had already landed by the time I opened them again. If it wasn't for my fellow Americans, blurry eyed and barely awake, I might have spent that night in the terminal. I had laid down on the carpet while my buddy arranged the transportation--half asleep.

I didn't want to get back up. Suddenly being taxied down the winding paths, too tired to grasp the shacks and repetitive flashes of society, we arrived at the seaside without a bushy long-tailed captain.

It was late. I don't remember how little we paid to get to Railay West, but what I do remember was the barefoot walk into the Andaman Sea to throw my bag into a foreign type of craft. The camera in my mind hit the record button then.

Our ferry was manned standing up with a ten-foot-long propeller extending from the stern steering the way. The wooden boat was nearly as long or longer. The bow of the long-tail has red and blue scarves tied to the extended nose to guarantee safe passage. They protect by homage to the sea goddesses that would spill their disciplines upon anyone if neglected (just as any woman would). The ferry was maybe thirty minutes in total, but after an approximate half-way point, jungle covered spires began to jet out of the water. From the shadows of the night, out loomed an old world. All around us like islands of rock tan treasure, and dark green pirate coves, our landscape became the recollection of stories layered beneath years of bedtime conditioning. In the wind on our faces, I could smell those dreams surfacing in the chopping of the water.

# *10*

Our long-tail beached on Railay West and, like Jonah, we were spit out of that whale into a tamer version of Nineveh. The friends that helped me borrow a shuttle (and the long-tail), then showed us to a good spot to take in from the night our first steaming bowl of spicy coconut milk curry.

Showing up on a beach doesn't make anyone legitimate. Buy the bungalow and store those things carried, but then what? See-saw, hee-haw? A small fish in a big pond loses its thunder going into the clouds. No one new walks in like they own the palace. In the eyes of the locals, they saw a couple of whiteys waiting to get burned red by the unbearable afternoon…and we did. Everyone has to swallow from the sea's salt a bit to feel really relaxed. I stepped in like the soul beggar needing *their* attention, but the reggae had already started. That welcome party is never ending and Southern Thailand is as close to Jamaica as I have ever been. The concrete jungle of Bangkok, in likeness to Babylon, on a whole seems depressed, but this is where the cool breeze speaks louder than the busy street. Love sounds from where the jungle met the ocean. Drinking at the Gecko Bar, we inquired about some ganja and the band that was playing tossed us their sack; telling *us* to roll a joint. I'll never live past how sloppy it was. We still smoked it.

Back on set, the band started playing again. Entranced, my mountain lion friend and I, amongst, writhed on fire into the early hours of the morning.

*11*

Traveling, I sometimes wake up and have no clue where I am. It's frightening for the moments it takes to reel in reality. Thailand. Ok. Here, I had walked into the lane where it seemed the Olympians were destined to be. I was wondering what I was really doing there. Underpowered and inexperienced, I got very self-aware. We had made our peace with the budeaters, smoking some of our suffering away, but those fishers of fish had textures on their hands that had never seen a day of softness. Looking at mine was the joke. I tried to keep my dignity though, by opting for the Jungle that first morning. It wouldn't really exist until we stepped into it.

When exploring south towards Pranang beach, the trail branches left or right. Right hand will take you to the seaside of Pranang, but the left-hand trail takes one into nuances of another book. My friend and I turned left.

That gradual honing-in that happens when entirely surrounded by mystery, inspired us to crouch like the human panther and quietly surprise rather than be surprised. Canopy clouds and buttress roots reach their fingers deep into the ground. We are foundationally the light-footed and the creature of lore. Creeping through the trails, the air was humid and my nose filled with the flora exhalation. Human muscles rippled and our feet grounded focus on the external surroundings. It felt as if our ears grow longer gathering nourishment solely from the clicks and hums of the jungle tunnel. Black was becoming color, and color was becoming black.

Up ahead, behind some trees along the trail there was a sound of a subtle scratching like leaves rustling. Everything else got quiet. I could see some movement maybe thirty yards away. As we got closer, clear as day, foraging through the leaf litter was a seven-foot long monitor lizard. Dragon-like in its appearance, its nose was to the ground snuffing around for whatever grubs, bugs or vertebrates it could find. Eyes set forward and locked on to what we were seeing, each step had to be quieter than the sound the lizard was making. Slowly moving out of the direct line of sight, the sweat from the humidity and tension was rolling off the skin with a pitter patter onto the ground. Coupled with the tension of the stalk, below the radar, there were thousands of tiny mosquitoes accumulating on our legs and arms. Those blood suckers were sucking it up and drinking it down in order to make ten thousand more! How maddening! It's impossible to sweat or swat them away without revealing our position. When an animal is found unaware, the first instinct should be to keep it that way and get closer…for good fun. Can you get closer?

Approximately, fifteen feet away from the lizard and just behind a tree, the itching from the mosquitoes began to climax. Lizard still didn't know human was there. Insects kept tempting the scratch and swat, but the monitor was still undisturbed. I wasn't. My vision almost blurred by the amount of itch and agitation...Forget it. Out I jumped! The lizard probably did too and bolted away crashing into some shrubs and rubber trees. I tore after him in tempo with Credence Clearwater's, *Running through the Jungle* like a slap-happy machete tear, through one-hundred percent humidity, just ahead of a vibrating swarm of very sly vampires.

We were then moving fast enough to be the surprised. Giving up on the chase, the thought of a rise out of the trees into the canopy breeze could blow our cares away. Winding our way up a slope we found a trail that led up the side of a rock spire. On our ascent, pushing through the foliage and branches, fully focused on the route, I looked up, right in time to avoid stumbling face first into the largest spider-web I have ever seen—smack dab in the middle was a palm sized weaver...

## "The dark-Side of the Web"

Whoa! Harvest-man.
Floppy daddy long legs,
You're no arachnid without cephalothorax.
Where are your eight eyes true to the hunter?

Maybe just too small to see...


The fear of us spiders
Comes from the soft pitter-patter
Of barbed claws up the naked arm in surprise
Tickling through flesh,
Sending repulsive shivers bone deep
Or in the low light, See the demon hanging in the corner
From her symbol of deception
In malignant repose.
It is an honest threat
Conscious creatures
Weavers of energy
She can feel your eyes.
They know when someone is watching,
Their segmented legs covered in bristles
Spinneret abdomen oozing silk
Flash, flurry, scuttle, scuttle!
She's coming to eat me!
Fangs piercing soft tissue
Violently injecting poisonous saliva
As the venom liquefied organs
I got packaged in her threaded coffin...


Pushing more delicately through the trees of unknown, eucalyptus, and shrubs, we finally got the view from our surroundings. Vertically oriented, the wind and rain had chiseled ribbons of teeth, of scaling stones. With all the bloodsuckers vanquished in the sun, it's haiku could be more than just felt . . .

Hatching rock
Egg tooth trees
Diamond nearly floats
Hatchling rock makes sound
Egg tooth trees chip out from earth
Deaf diamond light floats

Our bungalow came fully furnished with rats, geckos and bedbugs. The toilets didn't flush and we had to fill a bucket to pour it down. We interpreted the hose out of the wall as their version of toilet paper. It became acrobatic to clean a butt under such circumstances. We had to get through the mosquitoes and the spiders before we'd get to any panther.

"Good night, sleep tight.
Don't let the bedbugs bite."

# 12

*Days Ahead:*

Rather than retracing every step, we looked for new ones to tread. Ascending to the jungle spire to escape the sucking-insect hoard, we had taken a path upwards towards a rock face, while a different, shadier path remained unexplored. When we revisited that intersection, we went down a descending trail and reached a series of drop-off ledges. There were about six, one after the other. Each step in that cliff staircase was approximately ten or twelve feet tall. People prior had tied ropes to aid in the climb down, but it was more fun to find the footing ourselves. The route was chiseled out between two skyscraping walls, sheer on each side. The rock channel we were following finally gave way to a cathedral of light inside a chimney of limestone. Coming out of the narrows, we declined upon a tidal lagoon.

At the sea's level, rock nymphs and other flightless fairies had written their visions onto the stone template. Everywhere there was an ochre clay that stained its umber upon all that it touched and the soil itself became the artist's palate. I tried to sit down without painting a picture but couldn't.

The liquid aurora refracted its mothero-pearl on the overhanging inlets and like jungle gnomes we swam in the color spectrum zone with plenty of room left to paint o-as-is.

# *13*

REFINEMENT OF THE BODY

IN LIKENESS OF ROCKS

GATHERS NO MOSS

It was then the second year after I had started rock-climbing. Most frequently through high school, my friends and I put our hands into the chalk bag bouldering. I had arrived in Thailand, willing for more than I had practiced for. We had brought a rope and enough quick-draws to scale anything we wanted to, but it was still somewhat laughable how we did it that time.   After the morning would come, "What do you want to do today?"

"I don't know. How about we go bouldering?" Pause "Ya, it's too hot. We slept in again . . ." "Let's just get stoned and snorkel."

We weren't laid in pavement every day of course; we just needed that speech or something. Rock-climbing is not a loner sport by any means. It seems closer to *the* partnership. You gotta really want it or it can quickly become upending.

We had rented out a bungalow in between the East and West Railay beaches, so Tonsai, where the more serial rock killers are found, was a place we tended to visit rather than call "home base". This trip was the first time I started putting the sport climb in any kind of way. The both of us climbed tops around the 5.12a, but on lead we couldn't just walk up and flash 'em. (They kept their modesty). Without a guide, some of the anchors appeared very sketchy. A few are just aged slings of webbing through eyelets of an ancient lime.

After someone warms up on your project climb, you realize there never was any competition. Rock climbing boils down to the internal one. Everyone encourages each other. Those people I am exceptionally drawn to are the ones with the lay-back strength of a rock climber's personality. We all enjoyed the never-ending challenges found in a whole community built around the rock warrior's gymnasium. Before any selfish thoughts of achievement or progress, homage first to the locals who were the first to worship atop Thailand's pillars.

# *14*

There are these monkeys that come down to Pranang beach and hover about in the trees. They wait to steal everyone's leftovers. They pick through the trash and climb back to the treetops, find what goodies people didn't eat or the vendors couldn't sell, and promptly drop it back down on top of our heads. It's the birth place of profanity no doubt.

There is a reason why I like books. There is always time for reading because there is always the heat of the day next to a shady tree.

During the afternoon 'reading hours', I would read books such as J.D. Salinger and Tom Wolfe, Kerouac and Nietzsche. Given this unsettling setting of exploration, it impacted me greatly. I would read and reread them within their power to confront my soul. (I was always told that the eyes were the gateway to the soul. When I closed my eyes and I still saw light, I just figured that was my soul.) My lights were nourished by those tales and thoughts at the same time as I was being relieved of them. I have absolutely no need to retrace the stories I've read about in my daily walk. Their karmas are not mine, but books have such utility and intention to expand out our capacity for what is possible, and what to expect when there actually *is* a shared karma.

I don't know why I must get drunk to be at peace with some things. I'd like to change but it is a very unusual state of affairs we are mixed in as modern humans...People taking pictures every second, using cameras more than their minds. People living on sugar and caffeine while trodding upon the shoulders of the locals to get what they want from time. Safe to say, everyone wants to be someone special. From the location and the books, I gleaned inspiration like a sponge, grew legs, and set out on a new course for DNA.

I'm not writing a war story: I couldn't join the army. To me, it's an absurd and bloody battle of the heart to get a message to the brain. Any war story was first a lover's story gone wrong, right? Being young, with nothing substantial to fight for or protect yet, my friend and I were imprinting. I started to feel like a fenced in and territorial mess. As I see it, as I see myself, ignorance lives on because it follows by example, not because it is a fixed state of being. Observing a trap, we segregate into cliques for too long. It seems that the problem only gets worse. I observe and therefore participate in something called psychic pollution. Every scheming subconscious taps into the collective experience. The 'true-to-life' quantum existence has no concept of proximity. Sentient beings are affecting each other across the known and the unknown all the time.

Just sitting and eating breakfast, desperation was in our faces. Diseased feral cats and dogs were rampant and multiplying in the garbage. I have never been able to devote my attention into just getting laid. We had drinks one night with this group of girls from Sweden and these two dogs started going at it right next to the bar. They got stuck together and the male dog was entirely twisted the other direction yelping in pain driving pins and needles into the atmosphere. One of the Swedish girls began yelling for someone to help them! "Do something! Do something!" …"What?" I had no answer. Woman is an adventure unto herself, and as many travelers know, "Stay out of the countries at war with themselves." I can fain to be pretty diplomatic. The Taoists teach that the secret to longevity is to conserve, not preserve, the sexual output…It is apparent that 'all fall short of those highest places' trying to get there forcefully.

When I fain to be a musician (three musicians and a drummer), I see the dance must have a driven passion. When it is hard to even find a person syncopating the same song let alone one that is not just reciting something memorized, I get frustrated by feeling distant— Not all, but most real-life love stories I hear about are tragic. A few encounters of my own have crippled my ability to find what I needed in this world at that time. I won't do it again. I have always felt monogamous but when I get eaten on too many times to wake up repeatedly in the same state, I look on.

Yet again, the only way to heal the past is to follow through with the present. When the ghosts of memory spook the Now, Mowgli can't run away. Memory is the practice of visualization; it is a problem-solving practice. When the past catches me, I will always relive the entire experience to the end. The difference is revealed when after a week, sometimes up to an entire month of dream torture, my true-self becomes emboldened within those life impressions of the soul. I wake and become lucid. Instead of following the stream like a projector screen, I can choose to do it differently within that trauma-matic movie. The plot takes on a different ending and I get to become something I had always wished to see myself as within that particular experience. The intuition closes the door on that which drains me. I'm not saying we all should become delusional, but I am feeling much better by relearning how I should have done it better. I cannot carry any excessive weight because a pack's survival depends upon it. Karmas will bind too quickly and the cycles of life carry themselves out beyond the counter. I am just careful before I am carefree. By being so, I get to say that I am a man-cub without consuming shame. I find what I am given and take nothing more. Out on Pranang beach, in pure admiration of those topless European betties who had that Speedo confidence found wanting in hung-over societies, I felt I was gazing with something other than the generic lust. There is no replacement for the nudity of a confident woman, but all one must do is confide in the purer memory.

# 15

I was in the wave of a five-foot crest, and on each one I rose up . . . then dipped back down again. Beneath me was depth approaching on night and what I felt was the monsters coming out right below me. Never had I joined the ocean in such serious courtship this far from land. There are no breaks moving through the water, and I found myself needing the joy of strength in every swell of the midnight blue sea. Within any peace of mind, there are fearsome things just beneath the surface. I suspected them and accepted them with my own inevitable ending. I was without an oppressive worry of the ever-present fathoms of hungry living that would gladly dine on my corpse if I just happened to stop swimming. The water was warmer than the air, but every so often my feet would kick into a pocket of extra cold water. In practice of easing the breath, I relieved the hyperventilation. I felt too alive in the moment, and the sinusoidal wave continually rollercoastered me closer to an epitaph: barefoot and warm, far from shore, up and down, willing on that day. I was even swimming to the West just as the sun was setting on that surface balanced atop a cusp just before the point of no return. The Great Ocean would welcome me in the end regardless, and I was at that place that all things wash down to. My body felt strong and my skin was tan. I had summitted my experience and I could not see anything important between that moment and the moment that I would be swallowed by the insatiable salty water. The swan song sung a message to me, "In order to take one more step upon this carnivorous planet, something has to die for you to do so. Is it worth it to just be alive?" The sun posed as the giant falling globe that sends tracks of orange light across the planet's curves. All absorbing frequencies went into the rock but as if from the earth's own light, swirling browns and charismatic greens, sky blues and jewelry yellows rippled up and down into the waves to my dilated pupil as one great white light .

# *16*

## No Shirt, No Shoes, Yet Service

The second to the last night before we headed back to Bangkok, we made our way to our favorite drinking joint/tikihut called, "Jah Bar." Our Thai bartender-friend was named, Bäm. We met Bam one night after returning electric, while I was dressed up like a spoofy crocodile Dundee, beneath my dumpy hat and wearing a snake vertebrae necklace. I reached to my opposing shoulders so that my elbows came together in front of my face, and opened and closed them like a mouth, making alligator growls as was appropriate. He took one look at me and the widest laugh spread across his face. It was good fun and a sad prospect to be leaving so soon, but the night was still young and we had planned to get a traditional bamboo tattoo the very next day. We were at the last evening us two Idahoans could go into the Andaman sea or wash out the new ink—first ink. (Who my mountain lion friend is, I cannot rightfully say. I could not tell his story even though we've been friends for a long time.)

I got up to go check the music in the neighboring Gecko Bar, and I got the whistle from a group of girls. With a smile, I glanced their "holla" but after I returned with empty rapport, two of them followed me. It was a birthday. These girls had flown in from Australia to celebrate another day among the living and I had caught their eye passing by. Their accent caught my ear when they decided to sit and drink a beer. Quiet, pensive type, right? Yep, I am shy. On *om*-momentous occasions I feel like I am the confidant rather than the confident. I smoke too much, but I still know when I am crossing a great divide. My friend did most of the talking.

The birthday girl and I connected on that unspoken plane by both being somewhat reserved. A few drinks in and we didn't have to say a whole lot to each other listening to the charismatic play on the moment from my friend to hers. The most dazzling thing I have ever found is swimming at night in warm waters: bioluminescence. Nothing pollutes that light except the salt in your eyes. We had decided earlier to bring goggles this time around and watch those phosphorescent creatures express their glowing blue around our swimming movements as our heads were submerged. It came time and we cashed in. The invitation was accepted, and the four of us prepared to head for the starlight of Pranang. The water doesn't have to be deep to see your reflection in the darkest blue within that luminous spark of starry sky underwater. Needles of agitated life forms create wings of azure in the wake of any expression of the physical. We skinny dipped into the sands of timeless with a care to never fade, even if we did.

As the night pressed on, progressively each of our paths dwindled to sleep. Wide awake, the other three fell one by one to their rooms without any further thoughts for the night. For some unknown reason, when everyone around me goes to sleep, I wake up again. I was restless, goaded not by misgivings but by the wakefulness of the advent and a continued need for it. Musing unwound and I sought solitude.

# 17

IT WAS WELL INTO THE NIGHT,
AND I HAD TO SNEAK ABOUT
AS NOT TO GET CAUGHT
DURING THE OFF-LIMIT HOURS.

Well known to the inhabitants and visitors to the peninsula of Kräbi is a cave. This cave is visited frequently due to advertisement as an attraction and within it, is built a wooden walkway. Anyone can find easy access to explore it. The entrance to the cave is taller than wide, I'd say, twenty-five feet by ten. As the planks are set beneath your step, posted about three feet from the dirt floor, it takes on the form like a wooden tongue. Out of the gape in the hillside, a bristly jungle mustache grows on the face of a sleeping giant. He naps with his mouth open and a wooden tongue comes out of the jungle.

Around the first corner, the black swallowed everything; apart from the thin beam of light streaming from my cheap headlamp. The bulge and rib of a giant's palate are like bizarre forms of erosion; stone flesh grown from mineral tested time. Cascades of still life waterfalls, saliva slick and gleaming, statute the slow drips that deposit upon moment to moment's deposit.

The molars were very much like coming to the narrows near the back of a mouth, yet without a throat, it connected immediately to the stomach…I was consumed.

It was cool and wet as I climbed over the railing to the cave's floor. The echoes of the water were continuous and after each one, a vacuum of sound after a water drop dripped and rippled from the rafters as it seeped through the rock. It seemed as if anything that moved inside, could be heard from across the expanse. I spread out my bivy-sac much too loudly and slipped in. The light went off and the air became tense.

Wandering into the dark is like saying to yourself, "I wonder what's in there?" as if it's a curtain one can just brush aside. Groping for the edge of a dense cloth only to find that there is nothing to even push off of except deadly dark with deepening depth; a deepening awareness of how the silence breaks. It was an uneasy night. There were noises that could not be pin-pointed to the wind or waters passing across the vocal chords of the sleeping giant's innards. There were many things moving in the cave as I was trying to sleep. Several times, I would get up with a start and shine the light over my shoulder to catch what was crawling near me red handed . . . nothing. Or was it?

I could not stay more than five hours that night. A broken three, I would venture, were actually sleep. With turns and bouts of fictitious certainties only to find creatures too well camouflaged for my spot-light inquiries, I was more fatigued than rested. The sun would be coming up soon and with it, more humans hunting for their daily bread. I stayed as long as I could. I was on the other side of the fence, and began to understand why the animals hide from us. All that is left in the wake of Man is Air not suitable for the lung and Water to pollute the tongue. If you get discovered then you are either squashed, speared, bulleted or domesticated. I became fearful of the men, so I packed my things up and scurried like the fox back to my bungalow.

The next night, we got our tattoos and that graduated the incline from the academy of Kräbi. My tattoo was a symbol representing nothingness, surrounded by incoherent somethingness and how could I get upset about nothing? The smile that that thought brought to my face solidified my confidence for life.

# *18*

## BANGKOK

Jacques Cousteau's mother
booked us a hotel to stay
for one night
in the district of the Red Light.

***

In regards to Bangkok, all I can calmly say is, "I'm in a freaking zoo." Progress? Your water is black. The beggars on the street looked so messed, that help looked helpless. Everywhere, people had something to sell me. Everywhere, people had somewhere else to be. The wanderer was inherently without a natural sense of direction. I am food curious but that has been sitting there for too long by the looks of it. If you must break the surface first...I have trouble trusting it. Lunch was three hours ago and the memory of previous food poisoning kept me away from it. We quickly bought some strange spiny fruits and took refuge inside from the mayhem outside of our hotel. We read books until it got dark and Roxanne could really shine.

You like movies? The pirate is persistent. Myanmar sweats its labors into Thailand tourism and every other kiosk seems exactly the same. They do what they are told: knockoff-Rolex and ping-pong shows. (Fore anyone that doesn't know what a ping-pong show is, it's when a woman pops a ping-pong ball out of her va-g at maximum velocity . . . Sorry, I'm not that kind of hallelujah witness.) Every hour is happy hour! We accidentally went down the alley for the homosexualist, and we pretended to be gay as a hall-pass to ease through to the other side. Everywhere there was a new avenue for the sexual tourist. At dusk they opened like a hotel room vacancy above every strip club awaiting the little death of a man's sexual release . . . and the money that must follow. I couldn't buy in. It was much too expensive, so I slipped and slid through the desperate yearning for something more than what an individual can buy from the prostitution of his sister. No thanks.

Humans are the Frankenstein's of Nature's laboratory.
Thinking that they have a will of their own,
Yet always crying out, "Master, Master!"
Nature laughs back,
"You will never be like us."

I am glad the two of us didn't stay in Babylon very long. The color red is only one on the bow after a rain, and lifetimes are still simmered down and summed up to a scout troop's trip. *Om Namo Shivago, Kahp kun krahp.* I "smuggled" the remains of what acid I had leftover "hassle-free" all the way back home.

# 19

Near the dawn, there was a young boy who came to marvel at the skill and grace of an untamed hunting falcon. He would follow them through the forests and fields, across deserts and blinding tundra barrens.

One day, the boy followed a pair of desert falcons back to the eyrie. As one of the birds lofted upon the scrape high up on a cliff, the boy was intrigued to hear the screams of an eyas'. The parent bird had returned carrying something in its talons, but the boy couldn't make out from the sounds what exactly was going on up there. He was anchored in place by curiosity and venture. He waited for an opportunity to climb up to that ledge where he had heard those mysterious pitches emanate from.

The birds left for the day's evening hunt, and the boy crept out from some shrubs to the base of the rock. His body was kept limber and strong as a side-effect to his daily life. He tried to never go anywhere without a satchel for an opportunistic edible. After eating some ants, he climbed up, and peered over a ledge and the boy spied wide eyed with credulity at five small clumsy balls of down. The boy picked one up and smelled it. It showed no fear to him, so he took it home with him. The two became inseparable. They hunted together…. hiking and flying together as a team; an extension of their hearts beating together after the goal.

Soon after, the boy began to step out of his provincial days and his father handed him a gun. Having learned all that he needed about the quarry at hand he began to think of owning his own poultry shop. With his shotgun, he became so busy he made no time to mess around with his falcon. He could kill more than it could in a month, in a single week. So, he did. His shop was very successful. He practically set a new standard in his village's diet. It became odd to not have a bird on the table. The children began to expect it. Our now young man had his own pangs of conscience when he was reminded that the falcons weren't getting share and the populations were becoming low. It was going to be his business or the falcons. The grouse got dumped like an ugly breakup, as if a war was declared. Falcons haven't lost, but the pillage still took over.

Years down the road, the not so young man anymore loses his hearing from firing hand-cannons for so long. He still operates his business, but he has lost his taste for the marauding thunder-stick. He picks up a bow and arrow like he was young again but quickly loses interest because *he* hunts birds. He doesn't care to start all over again and is reminded of the deadly proficiency, next to the gun, the falcons of his boyhood had proven. He sees his desperate side in the relationship and asking what he must do to fix the situation, he learns that he must realign his allegiance from profit to companionship…Instead, the man stuffed his ears with hearing aids and plugs so that he couldn't hear his newest model shoot what was left of his dinner.

# 20

What a person decides through personal experience has "worth" is what that human values. Values determine morality. Morality *does not* exist until 'value' is placed on an item or an ideal. Anything that jeopardizes or damages that physicality or ideal becomes morally wrong. All that supports it is morally correct. Ethics try to apply morality to individuals en mass, yet coordination is still dependent upon a common *value*.

It tries to tell the truth in the story of the vermin. When an animal becomes a nuisance by threatening anything we value, that animal becomes demonized by solid fear and hatred.

There are sent out open invitations for its public slaughter. After it is extinct or nearly so, scientists begin to research it. With apparently new and multifaceted understanding, those knowing humans frequently yearn for its presence again. If it is not too late, the other extreme, preservation, recoils back in to varying degrees of success… Humans tend to coordinate upon a value that is not always the "best" one.

Homo sapiens are fickle to separate the spiritual and the physical, because every journey immediately becomes a spiritual one, when the mortal sees its ending. I do feel parasympathetic, yet I don't understand our story without some form of psychedelic pressure.

It does become very interesting how Moses' edition of Genesis recounts a story about a pair of naked hunter-gatherers living in perfect harmony with the plant and animal world. They end up tasting from a fruit that possessed a knowledge, which in-turn cursed them to toil with clothing and the land as farmers. The way back to their previous harmonies was shut forever more…

These animals, plants and thoughts have become inseparable from real life, and are still an open median for finding your place in it all. Because we have adopted our ancestor's new style of subsistence (farming) and what has been born from the fruits of knowledge thereafter, it just might be that we are bound to the fate of their biblical soothsayers.

Ignorance isn't bliss. What do you Value? Once the falcon was viewed as more than just a competitor for pheasants, chicken and grouse, the bounty was lifted off its head, and it again became something that could influence antiquity. The unchecked persecution of the "evil" transmuted into something priceless. How my American ancestors have walked is linked behind the drywall and under the carpeting through the skeletons of our own creations. Shoveling things like our use of falcons and psychedelics into the closet to post a sign, "do not enter" is not where I'm coming from. Granted, psychedelics act volatile and unpredictable like a bear, but that is why both the bear and the plants have been used as rites of passage, as indicators of the inner roadblocks. I don't think it should be an immoral dilemma, but it is. I'm calling it, "Mortal Morality."

# *21*

## SELF-INTRODUCTION

Today is my birthday! I laughed. Very shortly after my mother named me Isaac. Orphaned in my own meadows, the animals came to know me as Mowgli, yet I only know myself as Ishmael. In honor of Herman Melville, call me Mowgli. I am a hermit by my profession and a minimalist by trade. I aimed to be enlightened, but I am still, as all three, the worst person I will ever know. I came through into this birthday unconscious and therefore hold no true understanding.

Because it is my birthday today, we all have to wonder how old I am. When considering the age of something it is from its birth that we measure the number of the years old. So, if we all have the same origin, the same birthday (creation, big bang, alien insemination, etc.), we actually become the elder of that, which has come before us. If something died two hundred and fifty years ago, on the frontier of things, I am in fact two hundred and fifty years older than they are. Happy Birthday.

Acknowledging that need to learn from those that have come before, is nonpareil, but it is still *us* who must become the pioneers.

To do this, it does not take an "old age" not even sage when so called magic—even miracles—can't be said to be something that exists, in and of themselves. It has always been that something in-between. It's quite easy to see that our magic as humans exists betwixt the human to human, human to plant, to star, to planet, to animal on a high. After all the wonder seemingly shifts and evaporates too quickly, we get left as merely observers: plant to plant, rock to rock, star to planet, planet to star, other human to another human. I say this is the very quality that makes us what we are. It makes every single one of us into alchemists: observers becoming creators, stirring soups with spears.

My problem is, I never agreed to be such a tool user. After shedding the heavy skin, what I have come to value is the Dreamtime and the Story. The moral of this story is to never live a boring one, and the hypothesis of the story is that the nighttime and daytime dream is the only thing that has the ability to healthily interact within and among all other messages on morality.

Try to never take your eyes off the storyteller lest he sell something one can't afford. I do have a hidden agenda. A nice word for it is prosperity...Peace of mind proper just goes well with it. I have had trouble finding it. The mean word "dream" has many ambiguous meanings and I imply all of them.

This contagious Western World insists upon operating by the clock, but all the while Albert Camus' Absurdity sneers at those losing sleep . . . Only the dreamer is able to sneer back. Complexity becomes just a conglomeration of simplicities. It becomes entirely possible to deconstruct with the intention of dissection (i.e. chemistry, psychedelics, fasting, abstinence, hunting) in order that the Dream may be put back together and function out clearer than how it initially began. Every species has a story it wants to tell me. Every creature on this planet has its own dream. Seeing dreams through and adhering to the story faithfully is the balancing act of the storyteller. If I go too long without harmonious synchronicity from the inner and outer lights, discord sounds loudest, and I then begin to lose the desire to be.

# 22

## IDAHO STATE UNIVERSITY

Preceding these travels, wolf-brother and I had taken an oath to never go to college. I know now that the lingering taste of debt in my mouth was worth it, but I still don't have to like it. The elder generation offers everything and the new one wants nothing to do with it except on credit. My peers have scared me defiant because of what we have missed. We sense the error, yet most of us can't say it out loud without coming off paranoid or rambling on. The two of us wanted to find the backbone of a sailor's life; something that could compare with Herman Melville's poetic merit. We still be sailing, but without any previous freelance experience, I'm not sure I would have ever enrolled. I graduated high school with no preparedness for such a course, yet changes to a preconceived journey, rips through the barrier of comfort and brings forth what seems natural when it actually arrives. Raw experience is still the way to find a white whale, and I was listening to what was before me foremast.

I expected to not know what would happen. I had bought myself some time, but most frequently college is just seeking approval. The teachers don't keep up with the learning that happens there, and capital Ideas get thrown into the dark.

"What does the Ph.D say to the other Ph.D?"

"Would you like fries with that?"

"Oh, I graduated in metaphysics and resorted to teaching. It didn't pay enough so I got a job here."

All the while the patron Ph.D is staring blankly. With manipulated, "Ya, I'll take fries," he shares his food with the trash bin.

The grade point average measures way too low. Learning from books has to be about an individual's passion. Without it, one should not be in this type of school, but in the wildernesses finding out what that is. I couldn't take too many of my teachers so seriously along because I had just gotten through learning that to be prolongedly barefoot was one of the single most keys to my function. As a person who needs validation of the soul more than a raise, I cry out loud when I hear that rubber and asphalt have been between the animal and the dirt their entire lives! Health has required something different as found in reflexology. To not participate within the natural contours of the planet cripples an entire population. Where is that sweet chariot of fire to swing low and scoop everyone out of their living hell? Education demands that the elders show us a better way, but when they have neglected the basics, I listen only with a grain of salt in the next generation's wound. It takes a whole heart to understand the details of universal respect and maintain what is due to those that teach, yet I don't expect many grasp more than what they are told, solely based upon the rarity of a person who is actually happy and vibrating health.

What is knowledge good for if it does not foster either? Idyllic University teaches tranquil diversity. To me that is known as *zen,* the love language of Japan.

# *23*

## 北海道

### WEST OF THE 44TH DEGREE
### HOKKAIDO, JAPAN

After my first year of college, I saw an opportunity to do
something I had always wanted to do. I had no money, so I
worked with it to take out a school loan and teach English
for two weeks in southern Japan. Although, the entire trip
would be a little over two and a half months.

I would fly into northern Japan and travel south through the mainland until the smaller southern island of Kyushu; where I would then teach English. Rather than buying an "expensive" rail pass and hostel, I opted to hitchhike and sleep outside wherever I went, even if it meant I had to walk. If I had to walk, I could just become more like the traveling poet, Basho. When I was a junior in high school, I participated in something called the Sister City Exchange Program. I stayed with a host family for two weeks on the northern island of Hokkaido. The Sister City to Pocatello, Idaho is Iwamizawa, Japan.

I had so much fun with the family I home stayed with that I decided to continue the connection I felt for them and visit them once more. They were the ones that picked me up from the airport in Sapporo and I began my next two weeks in Hokkaido as a Japanese housewife.

# 24

When the jet hits bad, it means lag. The amount of Japanese I was supposed to relay dwarfed what I actually knew. I had my few moments of clairvoyance, but the task of keeping up with a suppose'd learne'd stranger's language on top of the need for the entertainer's critiqued response, at first, caused in me the sensation of no feeling at all. Beneath the clouded sun, my mind went numb. Even my English played a gutter ball. The first week there, I was coerced into going to an aerobics class with my host mother. "But all of my clothes are in the laundry!" I insisted. Instead of an escape, she pulled out this tee-shirt that an exchange student of the past had brought for her son. It was extra small and all white with only the American flag front and center. I showed up jet lagged as never before to do aerobics in a Japanese diction I had never learned. Whatever . . . I had American pride on my side! The music went. The steps were stepping, and the punches were punching. Now we're turning. Ok, forward, back, but I was so behind and out of step, left alone, the only non-Japanese person in the class, all inquisitive eyes were doing the peripheral on me. Curious they are! I was spotlighted from every angle due to the mirrors surrounding what appeared to be 'me' in a self-conscious costume. After it was over, I received no more pressure to go to any more aerobics classes.

Three "daze" into the trip, I was hired on and paid under the table to work the family farm. I could earn some extra traveling money for the journey still ahead of me. My working hours were 9:30-4:30pm. I was paid 1000 yen per hour which was roughly ten dollars per hour in 2008.

To start the job, trays of sprouted rice were hauled out of the mini-dome greenhouses into the bed of a truck. Each greenhouse was approximately sixty feet long by twenty feet wide and tall enough to walk upright comfortably in the center of them. The trays of rice were watered by a suspended sprinkler system and filled about seven domes total. After the 1'x2' plastic trays were stacked in the back of a white Tonka truck, they were then transported to some flooded fields a few miles away.

Each individual rice plant is approximately the width of the ring finger and six or seven inches tall. The plants themselves look similar to a broad-leafed crab grass, only with a brighter and more upright green.

My first impression was that they were delicate but the trays were stacked atop each other with gusto and as they piled higher and higher, I had to check the face of my Japanese counterpart to reassure myself that the plants were that hardy. They huddled squished together as if saying their farewells before they had to be planted a distant six inches away from each other.

Many rice plantations in Japan still subsist by planting rice by hand, but many farms have innovated beyond the traditional style to straighten their spines some. Machines can never improve upon the beauty of an antiquity, but the plants I was tending were traveling to meet the mechanical hand. My host family's tractor had columns that resembled a rectangular shelving unit on the front, the left and right sides. The driver was positioned behind and between the units and as he drove along the perimeter, he continually fed the trays of sprouts from the shelves into the lowest compartment. They were then mechanically lifted out individually from the plastic tray and inserted into the ground. It reminded me of parallel cookie cutters rolled across a watery piece of dough. Instead of gingerbread men, there was a row of upright plants in the tread of a liquid road after the tractor had passed by. My job was to load up the trays of rice first into the trucks and then onto the shelves of the tractor as he made periodic pits stops to reload his clips. I then finished by stacking the spent trays to be reused the next season.

I was treated fairly lax due to my status, and everyone seemed to be in a healthy relationship with the work that needed to be done anyways. I got bit by their large "not-too-keen-on-strangers" husky dog, named Chitah. I was plenty smoothed out with the first "not-soonto-be-last" glass of *shochu,* sweet potato *sake.* However, all the motherly figures wanted to water it down till it drowned. The grandfather was on my side and with a wide and toothy laugh, he tossed in an extra sympathetic slosh. Drinking *shochu,* jabbing, and lounging in their living room was apparent as the afterwork ritual. I was gazed and prodded at with Japanese by the expectant and wide-eyed familiars to their own home while I squinted from the outside trying to understand what they were even saying. I was in the rigorous first week of a challenging new exercise program. My mind clung to anything that seemed familiar as the world was turned inside out of the norm. There was a nagging sense of desperation because everything, including what was thought to be mundane, transfigured into associative foreignness. I got so overstimulated that I often appeared empty. That was a frequent condition experienced before, during and after planting Japan's rice into this story. It was evident that they were growing me as well.

# 25

## IRASHAIMASEN DOZO!

I admit, I eventually found my way to an aisle with the beer—surrounded by hello kitty bubbles just ready to gift wrap something extra nice…The grocery stores had these motion detecting jukeboxes that sang little jingles from commercials as people walked by. I didn't understand what they were selling, but to be honest, I felt they contributed to my selection. Asahi and Sapporo called out in liquid transcendence. I was still measured one year younger than Japan's age limit of twenty, but they were unwilling to passport me. Despising how alcohol is most commonly the scapegoat, yet in defense, many of the Japanese television programs just like to see what happens when 'appliances' are dropped out of a helicopter (trying to bounce them off trampolines).

Household items did get some air! The generation I come from has seen its share of Power Rangers on Saturday morning cartoons, but the Japanese have taken it to the next level. They calculated how many 8"x11" pieces of paper it would take to photocopy and tape together to make a real life-sized paper figurine of a character after it had morphed into its battle height; to dwarf the surrounding city. They taped them all together like scientists and suspended it from a crane to tower above a Tokyo. Snapshot from a coffee shop, "What's that behind you!" It was fantastic. Everyone loved it, and I loved them. The furniture stores have these massage chairs that could be tested out for free. Every time my family and I went into the malls, the question was asked, *"Massa-ji chei-a-?" "Hai"*

There seemed to be a television on wherever we went. TV's are so filled with people elected to be hosts of something important. Every once in a while, there are those gems that stream from the tube with no critic invoking break in their performance. It feels like a confession to openly brawl with that side of us that has no grace; shaking mid-pose like a minute glitch in the consciousness of flow. The glitches become somehow justified as a part of the dynamic play. I watch in assumed full color upside down and inverted on the screen interpreted inside of my brain. Practice is too often waiting for the stars to realign. I will often bide time and call it how I've spent it, meditation. Proper posture is not necessarily required. I do admit that it's not very interesting watching someone in the audience stare at a portal on the wall. *Cognito ergo sum*. "I think therefore there is"... a rat's nest of a problem. Whether the time gets spent or not the result seems to be the same: life is diagnosable looney. We sit in the darkness's looking out of our recesses so that what is truly light and luminous will appear apparent—convincing me that humans need the caves Mowgli originated from. The shadows of Form cast on the walls comfort the oblivion encountered when gazing at what cruelty is around them. All domestic life, even with its natural "outings," quickly begins to feel confining. It was only two weeks before the pining for the adventure that I had originally planned became unbearable. I wasn't in the place that had what I needed to find for myself, before the journey ended and I would start to teach English.

The details of time threaten to bog down even the worst of stories, so I round down. I do not ever intend censorship, in order to make a point to all this, quite the opposite I suppose. I travel a lot, but I shy from arrogant personalities that buff their fingernails about all the places they've been. I see it first as a syndrome to travel. There is an ever-present question, "Where is home?" How can there be credibility to be constantly driven from every place encountered, only to find the very same feeling detected from the last effort at "permanent" refuge. The detested feeling is that one doesn't belong whole-heartedly. It is important to be so, broken pieces and all. When the development of these feelings culture, it is evident that the wrong questions were being asked. Instead of inquiring, "Where is home?" look to the horizon. Only then do I become more aligned with the nomadic heart. When I silence the wrong questions, I get to hold what is dear to me as something like an ether or an all-pervasive rainbow, that has its home in all places but could never ever last forever in any one of these alone. After it rains, the renewed color shines brightest but then fades away.

My host-mother refused to let me leave her side as a hitchhiker, so she bought me a train ticket that took me south enough to comfort her misgivings. *"Abunai!"* she would tell me. "It's dangerous! Japan is not like it used to be. It's not safe!" (In line with the kind of talk that all mothers advise even for their adopted children.) That's why I couldn't ignore the contrast. It may be different for a woman than it is for a male, but mancub still has to leave the wolf-mother's cave to find grounding in this impermanence.

# 26

 6.9.08

To offer some characterization, from the eyes of the Japanese, I must have seemed very strange. White people wandering around turning brown from living out of backpacks isn't that uncommon and well known to occur.

Still, there is this flying curiosity when you actually meet people like this. In myself, from my eyes, it's as if I was still that child glued to the window at the sight and sundry of any vagabond. While I was in Thailand, my hair was barely long enough for a ponytail nubbin, but after a year had passed by, without knowing the barbershop, it had grown below my shoulders. I still always wore my dumpy fisherman hat that had a wire brim, making it easily compactable. Several times, the shock of taking off my hat caused double-take and a slight swerve--my long hair having been hidden. I had a hoop nose ring through my left nostril and wore shorts frequently, but when it did get cool enough, I put on my black running thermals beneath them. Through lingering pictures of adapted fashions, generations chronically inspire the furrowing of the brow in face of the previous one. It is an embarrassment to have harbored such a heathen in a clean and Shinto home. Whatever input I may have had, I felt I was a Japanese creation before I had even gotten there.

Sitting in the train from Iwamizawa to Tomakomai, I started the "real" trip. The high school monkeys were being pranksters, which made me smile. They kept chain-smoking cigarettes and filling plastic bags with any liquid they could lay their scheming hands on. After tying a knot in it, they threw it at the passer-bys out the window. I knew that it could have been me, just as well, getting hit by their *bandar-log* ravings. NOTICE ME! I wanted to be less inhibited too, but I was too preoccupied. The train ride was soon over with the turning of a page. When the train stopped, the doors opened, and some of the patrons scuttled off onto the platform at Tomakomai. I was one of them. I was without anything alluring yet to smell. So, I followed my ears. Waves.

I had to smile at that first vision overlooking the southern coast of the volcanic island string called, "The Land of the Rising Sun." The day broke open with every sense gathered together in union. Lively and vivid, they feasted on the symphony of the natural dynamo: rolling tumult of overcast whites and blues, salty air zealous to ionize the lungs, mixed with the cool breath of a westward instrumentation. The waves played as alternating cadences to the rushing and receding tracheal winds. Visual music that breathed; brought in with my mouth wide open to swallow and recycle benign off-gases the other living organisms exhaled.

Can we trust our gizzards? We don't have to, but the dream *is* real. The fates and famines have favored and feasted down-to-earth.

# 27

I sought the kanji for the next city I needed to get to from an interstate sign (both in English and Japanese) suspended above the roadway. 室蘭. Muroran.

Using a black marker on a thin piece of white cardboard, I copied the intricate crow's feet down as best I could.

On the southern border of Hokkaido, I paid to board a ferry that would take me across to the mainland, Honshu. I had six hours to wait there before the boat would arrive.

Luckily, my host mother had packed me a bento lunch and I relaxed into it; munching till the sun set.

The boat arrived and docked its station. There wasn't a long line, it being nearly seven pm on the pier waiting to board the ferry. Upon entering the vessel, I lingered against one of the hand railings to watch the sailors and their tasks for departure. Hokkaido's lights faded slowly away. When the transition from land to sea were finished, I found my way curiously inside. Uneventfully, I laid down to go to sleep in the community cabin with a dozen or so other Japanese on the carpeted flooring. The lights never completely dimmed and the sleep was intermittent, filled with scattered thoughts and wild musing about here, there, and everywhere. "It's good to carry at least a few coins for the ferryman, just as a precaution to keep oneself from getting left on the wrong side of the eternal channel."

Aomori-shi is a gateway town to the northern most horseshoe shaped bay of Honshu. A massive glass monument greets the revived from the night into a bright 7 o'clock sunny morning. With a ten-dollar taxi ride to get into the skirts of the city, I walked from that geometric architecture to Aomori Park. In the early morning shade, I took a stray-cat nap on a bench with the other Japanese transients not far off. The difference between those homeless and I is that I carried my "house" upon my back like a turtle from cartoons. I could always take my shell off.

The inventory of my bag didn't make me feel as if I was over-equipped:

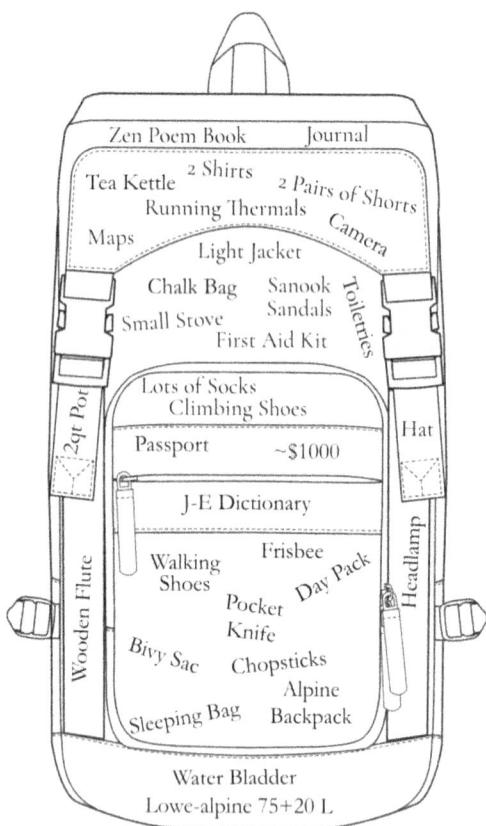

Zen Poem Book    Journal
Tea Kettle   2 Shirts
             2 Pairs of Shorts
Running Thermals
Maps                 Camera
       Light Jacket
    Chalk Bag    Sanook
                 Sandals      Toiletries
    Small Stove
         First Aid Kit
    Lots of Socks
       Climbing Shoes
2qt Pot  Passport     ~$1000    Hat

       J-E Dictionary

           Frisbee
    Walking          Day Pack
Wooden Flute  Shoes
              Pocket             Headlamp
              Knife
    Bivy Sac
           Chopsticks
                  Alpine
    Sleeping Bag   Backpack
       Water Bladder
    Lowe-alpine 75+20 L

Slow and steady. I didn't have any business lingering as they may do in that park. After I napped with my house as my pillow, I started walking.

From sea level to go inland everything is uphill. At the first real summit looking out across the basin of Aomori city, I came upon a marble shrine engraved with music staff and jingle. With the touch of a button it jangled.

I looked up, thumbs up, and accepted number two hitchhike of the trip.

# 28

# 山登

## MOUNTAIN CLIMBING

On the northern island of Hokkaido, during my free time over the previous two weeks, I had hiked over some strange creeks, up muddy slopes, and walls of bamboo, through fog blanketed saddles picking up cicada stowaways along the ridges. I had the brain and the blood for some more of that. I tried sharing that with the middle-aged man that had just picked me up, dressed in blues and browns. I said enough for him to hear the level of Japanese I could and could not convey. During the drive my eyes went out the window for a place I might hike up and sleep that night. I rolled my window down without asking. Having walked most of the day, the sun was casting long shadows on a rich and lush deciduous sea of trees blurring by, just outside of arms reach. The smells of the ocean were being replaced with a cleansed scent of forest decay. It was cool and nourishing to the brain and the blood that saturates it. Signs started appearing: *Ropu-Wei*, Rope-Way. It was a gondola ride up to a lookout point atop the mountain, *Hakkoda-san* (Mount Hakkoda). *"Koko ga ii desu. Onagaishimasu."* With a bow and a sincere *Arigato Gozaimashita,* we departed. I walked up to the service building for the *Ropu-Wei* Gondola...I thought to myself, "They would have a map in the least."

The mountains of northern Japan are dense with low growing bamboo that are nearly impassable. A gondola ride before more trudging sounded comforting. I paid one-thousand *yen* for a one-way ticket. From the maps provided by the receptionist, I saw that there was another five or six more kilometers up and down three more peaks after the gondola docked. Anywhere along those trails I could set up my sleeping bag for the night. The weather was bright and sunny, and I didn't doubt that the night would be the same. I stepped onto the cable car accompanied by another Japanese couple and the gondola guide. Lift off.

---

The very first time I had taken a solo venture in Iwamizawa. I was on a bicycle and I came upon a hill where a road curiously switch-backed up to a hedgerow bordering a plateau. I hiked up to the trees making way for the road and peeking around them to the right side of the path was a fox.

Kitsune. In Japan, after a fox has lived for one thousand years, he grows eight more tails and can turn invisible on command. He turned and disappeared like a nine-tails in training, and left me with a sense of significance. Fox is the messenger of one of the most popular Shinto deities, *Inari-sama,* the god of agriculture. When I stepped between the horticulture, I found myself looking out across an overgrown horse track. Everywhere the grass had taken over because the races beneath the stadium had come to an end. I climbed up a ladder to one of the towers built within the oval, but the door was locked. I went back down from there and started noticing an extensive amount of birds. Lots-lots of birds! "Wait a minute, those are hawks!" They were lining the poles and filling the sky, oddly, in amongst them--crows; more than could be counted. Trees were blooming in bodacious contrast to the carpet of hawk and crow feathers I was treading. I picked through them like I was going to make a headdress. I filled my pockets like a sugar addict in a free candy store. It seemed like I had been . . . chosen (and how afraid we all should be of that complex.) I was there to find purpose but Mowgli was being taken out of proportion. My journal says, "I am supposed to be here or I am crazy," which is a down play to that momentary *feeling.* I went home that evening and slipped up into my room like I had the King's *Ankus* to other men. I shared my treasure with my host family, and they laughed. Derby track? "The dump is on the other side of the hill." Shattered, I knew where I stood . . . on the other side of that hill. I sent the feathers back by throwing them into my trash bin.

## MOUNTAIN EXPO

*i hiked a few peaks and went to sleep. in
this noisy, sorta spooky shack at the base
of* o-dake *("the big peak") in the
morning, climbed off that beast to* suka-
yu onsen. *hiked a bit further then caught
a ride with an english speaking hashi. who
had backpacked through south america,
egypt, america . . . he was on his way to .
. . kanji . . . and i was on my way to
hachino-he. split ways and went towards .
. .kanji . . . caught a ride by this cellphone
repair guy in a rental hybrid honda all the
way back around to hachino-he. slept near
a lake when i walked the wrong way for
five kilometers. after drinking some sake.
(end journal entry)*

I wrote a sign to go to *Kuji,* which is a place I randomly chose, but got taken for a better ride to a better view: *Kitayama-zaki* (north-mountain outcropping).

Northern Japan is still a well-cultivated *bonsai* forest. I saw the first master of that art on a double-arched, rock outcropping of Kitayamazaki with *matsu* pine trees drooling all over his old, wind chiseled face. The receding hairline forests drank from the ocean's fountainhead while the trees always seemed to be reaching out for something over the watery horizon.

After I was dropped off somewhere unknown along the coast, I downed the rest of my *sake* and watched the surf. At the end of the day, the tide was coming in on a rock I was sitting on. I was testing myself to see how close I would let the water get to me before getting up and out of splashing distance.

"Uh oh, this one looks like it might make it!"

"Awwww, too little too early..."

Sure enough, the water ebbed closer and closer like it was scouting the distance with its good eye, then WAAM! I got swamped by a big one. After drying partially out on a different rock, I was reunited with wonder.

I am sitting on the same bivy-sac ready to tuck in for the night to watch what it means to be in the country to be the first to meet a new day. I may go rock climbing tomorrow or I may hitch to the end of this island. I can leaf litter it all with an unadorned spontaneity or I could just never move again.

# 29

## 6.13.08

### FRIDAY THE 13TH

I pulled out my climbing shoes on the beach and went bouldering. The rock crumbled and I got clobbered in the face when a hold broke . . . At that instant, I wasn't entirely unconscious of the *possibility* of it happening, but it got me when I let it take all my weight. It gave my eyebrow a mean gash in it and a meager cut in my nose. Granted though, it couldn't have been any closer to my eyes. I guess that's what I get for pioneering…I stayed north for a few days hiking to and from a rest area called, Taro, and the seaside, for minor provisions. Going back and forth between the two, I got lost in this book of zen poems I was reading; the strange sounds of birds I couldn't identify and little white and yellow flowers falling off blooming trees in amongst the bamboo. I walked myself into a meditation. Counting steps as I inhaled to equal the same I took on the exhale. Upright, that walking tempo hypnotized me.

One day in my strange daydream, I found Site B. You know, the island where the dinosaurs were raised before they were shipped to "Jurassic Park"? All the lizards were gone but I could tell they had been there before. *Iwate,* the stone hand. I snuck inside the compound through a small unlocked window and opened doorways of spider-web curtains. I took pictures of the mini model architectures that showed the grand plans. It was a formidable vision. Expecting to find prehistory, though I couldn't find any signs of struggle. Looking at all of it in ruins was melancholic. It once represented excitement for a future that never came to past but just got covered up in dust and ground cover. I hoped to be aligned to that Ian Malcom saying, "Life will find a way".

The day I decided to continue hitchhiking, those of us in Japan were hit with an earthquake, *jishin.* I thought someone was getting attacked in-*si*-de a *bu*-il-*di*-ng at that rest center I mentioned. I was looking up the kanji for "south" in my dictionary when the doors of the building started rattling wildly, making weird sounds like wailing. The whole mountain was shaking, and everyone was glancing gasps to one another! YIPPY-AI-EI-KO! Silence.

Continuing on, I walked from Taro on the wrong side of the road (right side) for hitch hiking, but because of my long hair, a lady thought I was a woman, went against the flow of traffic and picked me up. It was a short ride after she realized I was a dude. Hindsight, she may have thought I was injured from the earthquake.

When I was dropped off, I walked up to a Lawson gas station and loitering around were these two friends. When we engaged in conversation, I learned that they had their day off and were willing to give me a lift saying they wanted to show me "something nice" , as they put it. As a testimony of Japanese hospitality, we drove up to this temple, mosied around it, and gave thanks. There was even a statue commemorating Matsuo Basho and the journey he would take along that very road. I laughed when my new friends told me that the scariest bug on the planet is a butterfly.

> "*ichiban kowai mushi* . . . butterfly!
> *fuwa fuwa fuwa fuwa . . . ahhh!*"
> Hiroki and Testu-kun
> toured Chuson-ji
> afraid of bugs.

## 6.17.08

I made it south from Sendai to a few km outside of Mito in one day and four rides. The fourth ride, that took me nearly the entire way, was a fellow nineteen-year-old named, Mitsuyuki (January snow). He had *hoko-onchi* (no sense of direction) but wanted to find *jiyuu* (freedom). He was learning how to wet the reed of a saxophone. We had sushi together. I almost thought Mitsuyuki and I would be spending more time together looking for freedom, but

Mitsuyuki's nights were spent inside. I was afraid we would only find freedom of the heart an ideal and end out working six days a week making *ramen*. I will explore Mito a bit, but then I am heading towards Nagano! However I might say it, I don't really know where I am going either.

(two days later.)

There was another curious ride I had two days ago on my way to Mito. As I was talking with the driver, he offers up this cask of strawberries to eat. After he found out I was ignoring everything except plants, he declares in English, "Unberievaberu!" Ominously, he said, "You will find a new energy." (He also voiced something about a church, but kept fiddling with all his radio equipment and detachable microphones that were dangling around him as he drove. I was thoroughly confused who he was.) I was given the entire container of strawberries because he said he had already eaten one. Strange but true to his word, he showed me an empty container in his back seat. The birds here *are* amazing.

# 30

 6.19.08

## ZENKO-JI

I reached a new state of mind while walking through an area called, Takasaki: I have no pride. I only attract women that are mountain lions. I was tired from the bad—mainly short—night's sleep, Mayumi's son, Yuundai, deprived me of. He sleeps like an ogre in the states between consciousnesses. (I could have been convinced.) Before I was dropped off, she purred in my ear and caressed my neck. We were already stopped, so out I jumped…

Soon after, a bird picked me up near O-yama and dropped me off near Maebashi Central. From there I walked off into a thoughtless meditation. I found a ride from someone that had nothing else to do on his day off except drive me all the way to Nagano. I told him he didn't have to but he just kept on going. It was very scenic for sure. If you look back it feels like every road leads to Nagano's Zenko-ji. The city streets are like tributaries in a river flowing to and from the temple. I wandered through the gardens and sat next to the pond there.

Thoughts returned.

Having eaten enough *conbini* (convenience) *bento* (lunch), the "now" state is in regards to the need for the absence of that "trash heap" death in my diet. *Nagano-shi no Zenko-ji*. Purity? Fruit is only one of the gifts I can think of without an inheritable trauma. (I have accepted that Life requires to feast upon my own life's potential, but if our "meat" has no harm to karma then why do we pickle ourselves when we die?) Why do we pickle ourselves when we're alive? The tree holds out its hand with an apple inside. Is there a simpler beauty than accepting that gem? Wilder fruits have taught me to be content with less. When the dust clears, we are still left the only ones to blame.

"Excuse me! Excuse me! I ordered a Johnny Appleseed, I don't even know what this is?"

Because purities have the most luster, they are sought for first and become the most burdened by exploitation and thieves' profit. If nobility is in the action, can we not in turn become more noble? Nobility can indeed become something self-proclaimed, so were then the nobles really Noble? It becomes doubtable when thoughts go behind the scenes, leaving all things exposed . . . The Age of Nobility could be dead. I can't tell. I haven't poked one in the eye to see a cyclops yet.

I had nowhere to sleep in Nagano-shi, but I heard of these three temples lying in the hills above the city, so I packed up and raced a full moon from Zenkoji's azalea and koi garden.

charge throughout the night
we met with illumination
to the top of a mountain
through an apple valley
I followed it
though an apple orchard
to the top of a butterfly kingdom
(shake your head)
Fairies with their fairy magic
yoga opens my blood gates
owls open my dream gates
and the day is opened by the sun.

On the temple stairs
at Hoku-sha of Togakshi
rain stones sound
from the pagoda
that is my shelter
wings of a bat
spontaneous sight
catching wet bugs?
birds with wet wings
beetles with wet shell
man with wet suitcase?

I lost patience.
I made the journey to the three temples
giant cedars
through the bird sanctuaries
I feel like sitting but the moskeets
I feel like walking but both my feets
I wanted to know my mind but keep both of my bodies
wild
It was a liberating feeling to be able to liberate yourself
of feeling
by packing your things.

I planned at about every corner but was changed around every bend. The night before, I had planned to climb Togakshi-san and hit the *onsen* with a side of *soba*. As I found out, the mountain climbing was washed out by Japan's monsoon season, so I decided to head for Hakuba. I lifted my thumb out and the first car to approach, stopped. He was headed back to Nagano, but wanted to stop to taste of Togakshi's famous noodles (check, please.)

We passed my turn for Hakuba listening to him give me a history lesson. With my continuous nodding and affirming in partial understanding, I was dropped back in Nagano-shi approximately Zenko-ji. I set my heading for Joetsu. First, I got my daily *pan* from the bakery, and walked another five or six kilometers down the road.

I hitched three short rides towards the inland coast of Joetsu. During the second ride, we rounded a corner and the cloud cover broke, opening the splendor of Myoko-san. Before that point, all I wanted was a seaside rest and cleanse, for my clothing was way overdue. Instead, I changed directions towards climbing *this* mountain. The third ride was from a forty-two-yearold, truck driver heading all the way to Joetsu.

I could tell he knew some stories if (he wasn't already) drunk and allowed to be loud. I asked him to pull over when I thought we were close to Myoko-san.

A fog had blanketed everything since the first sighting. I couldn't see the direction of the mountain anymore. I asked this lady which way I could go to get there and I started a ruckus. Around ten people came out of their homes to see what was happening. "What!? He wants to climb Myokosan?" In the Japanese fashion, I got a map and a ride to the foot of the mountain. It turned out Myokosan has a ski resort and ski lifts that run in the winter. I thanked them all very much and continued up that ski slope on foot. I passed a few lodges looking homely. It was getting dark around seven thirty, but just before, the mosquitos claimed the hillsides. I decided to try the door to the next lodge I came to. It was locked. The second one though . . . unlocked! I took shelter from the swarms and slept on couch cushions in spite of cursing the blood suckers up the mountain. All for nothing and I wonder when I will learn, just be well. Life exists in a nutcase shell.

# *31*

 6.24.08

Alas, *yama-nobori*! I climbed Myoko-san in the morning sun and ate breakfast at the shrine that tops every peak. The grandpa that helped me up the mountain found me on the way back down it as well. He was out gathering bamboo shoots and actually came down from above me as I rested on the mountainside. I felt that during the hike, the wet plants were giving me shower enough but we bathed together in the community's *onsen* all the same. If only I could show them gratitude as gracefully as they did hosting me. After coffee and strawberries n' cream, I departed to catch a ride to Joetsu. I landed at a *sushi* restaurant then walked to the Sea of Japan.

I washed my dirty, dirty clothes for the first time since I began this journey, started writing and waited for the sun to set.

For as long I am in this world of plastic, this world of imbalanced surplus, "nothing" can actually matter; Coming down the beach was a Japanese clean-up crew spearing the trash clean through to the sand with pick-up sticks. The Kanji might look the same but China's garbage does cross the Sea. I know *wu-wei* (no-thing) has then been justified. I want to be hungry without a *conbini* to feed me. For sustenance and the unopened package of the Earth, it all needs to be washed because not only my spirit is affected by this world that demeans from the human synchronicity I just experienced. Convenience? My greatest inconveniences tend to be my favorite experiences. I know my little world is flawed and therefore I take it upon myself. Apart from the people, lately, all I feel like I know is plastic. I carry plastic because it is light. The clothes I wear are plastic, I wake up to my plastic bed, and more food from too many plastic bags…I am doomed to die the plastic death!

# *32*

My day began with empty
war-lording castles.
moon-gazing with Matsumoto
Now, it is ending
with dancing fireflies
river frogs,
on gurgling rocks
I feel like staring.

# 33

## 外人

### OUTSIDE PERSON

As soon as I left the Sea of Japan, I felt I was at a crossroads. I had to decide where I wanted to go next without relying on whim or chance. Through retrospect, I feel that I chose the wrong way.

The two choices I had before me were to either go see the red-faced monkeys that spend their winters chilling in hot pools or try to enter a Buddhist temple for an "internship" at the famous Eihei-ji…

Eihei-ji was very beautiful but not a success in terms of *Sangen-sha.* I felt opportunity and they tried to trick me into thinking that the guy in charge was telling me I couldn't enter at all. I kept trying. They wanted me to reserve my spot months in advance! (I was struggling, seeing myself as the only one there that had actually earned being there.) The one that came forward with "pseudo boss" written all over his face had no power to bend the rigid rule. I almost felt like crying while I was trying to under-stand, also later, while I was touring through it. I kept thinking, "I don't have to meet any masters. To them, I am just *gaijin* (outside person) not a fellow student." My meander through the temple was filled with a strange feeling of melancholic fantasy, but those monks…those monks weren't like monks at all. They were like secretaries surrounded by office equipment.

## 6.29.08

Kind of depressed, I drank a whole bottle of *sake* and had a *vodka* and lime paired with some *shochu* at this Jazz bar. I talked with these people for a while. I attempted to bum a cigarette from the bar tender's girlfriend. He wasn't too keen, so I figured there was no way I was going to be able to stay the night. Alcoholic Japanese girl, Tomo, likes heavy metal and bourbon. I went on a quest to find my own cigarettes and *ramen.* I found the smoke and a place to eat. I incensed my mind and my stomach but couldn't find a dry spot for my heave. I tried sleeping in the park. My bed . . . the worst sounding dream: wet and sticky plastic bag with heavy rain drops intermittently pounding my ears, noisy streets, and an abrupt mooring; hair in my face catching on everything that zips, the backwash smell of my breath because this "tent" is too close to my face!

It got light by the time I crawled like a reincarnated toad beneath a parking garage, broke open my bag of peanuts in the shell and passed out on the cement, sick and homeless.

When I awoke, all I wanted to do was throw up and die. I looked rough. It was still raining. I didn't want to walk through town. I didn't want drag my house around. If it'd ever stop acid raining, I'd probably hitch to Kyoto, but right now, the sky keeps drowning out the plastic world…This damn peanut taste is in my nose! So, I changed. . .to the American Spirit brand on my cigarettes.

Trucks with gusto
take the hat right off your head.
Don't wait for the bald spot
to show up.
This guy was sitting on a street corner asking
people for more than a quarter.
"I walked across an ocean,"
I say to him in Japanese everyone laughed.
He didn't, so
I just laughed at him too.

"I don't actually feel like hitchhiking." So, I wandered through a cafeteria in a small mall and some middle-school girls made a quick, surprised look at me. I did the same and "freaked" them out. All three did an apologetic *asumimasen* head-bob, but the twenty or so people watching without noticing the cause of my behavior, bore down on me like a white-head on somebody's face. Good humor lies on a boundary line. I crossed it and went to sulk under a bridge like a troll pissed off by all the goats and their kids. Like children in that candy store, they had overflowing pockets without a story to see. Thailand planted a seed. Japan's rainy season was watering gold on it. Where could it bear fruit? Does fire ever blossom? Yeah . . . in the fruiting body of a goliath mushroom cloud. Hold your tongue and say, "Apple." *Neko jita.* Cat got your tongue? The cat's tongue in Japan means you can't drink hot liquids . . . asshole. Alternatively, *Hahna* means flower. *Hee* means fire. *Hahna+Hee=Hahnabee*, 花 ＋火＝花火, the Japanese word for fireworks.

## "Hallelujah,"

I heard there once were wolves in this land,
I saw there once were magnificent monsters . . .
"but where?"
The world seems to be that dead prehistoric timber-wolf
Remembered only by stealthy goshawks.
We are way too under-organized for such crimes.
True challenge is matched with solitude,
Looking for beasts that have already been killed off.
Still, the Japanese have that something to protect.
Any animal could play with the frogs,
If we weren't endangered in so many other places.
"Now there is a *gaijin* that knows how to use chopsticks."
"If only I wasn't so left-handed."

# 34

# 一期一会

ONCE IN A LIFETIME'S CHANCE MEETING.

The sky had started pouring rain capriciously on a hike, so I jumped on a train to this random town and compulsively got off of it . . . The prayer beads I found earlier that day, had a sticker on them I hadn't noticed: "As-seen-on-tv." It affected me deeply and I threw those *ju-ju* beads in the gutter. I got lost, not only physically but spiritually in a way. I found a park with a pavilion and started journaling in my sleeping bag. I decided that from then on, I wouldn't trust anything without confirming from within then without. I would take the ride respectively from my own body breathing and stretching, observing as I go. I can't be too attached to trinkets.

As I was spread out, about to fall asleep, a group of people found me sleeping under that pavilion in the town I didn't know the name of. A Jamaican cook and two others, each with a girl on their arm, walked up and shook me awake. I sat up and all six got this wild surprised look on their faces. "Weaaaww!" (not being exactly what they were expecting peeling out of my bivouac cacoon.)

I'm fluent in Japanese as some of them are in English and the conversation meets somewhere near the middle or not much at all. We tried and met. Shortly, they had to take the girls home and all wished me a good night. I laid back down and closed my eyes to continue my meandering dream. Not long after they left, I was suddenly awoken again to, "Izaaku! Izaaku! We feel you smoke weed!" We talked about the three-stringed, *shamisen* guitars. I asked him about all the reggae I had been hearing and the cook pulled out the 'Toots and the Maytal's song, *Pomp and Pride* as the ringtone to his phone. He said he had been to Jamaica and learned to cook the local food. We decided to hang out again the next day, eat some Jamaican food, and the four of us go soak in an *onsen* together.

After they left that night, I decided to go for a "stroll" around the city late at night. I ventured to the seaside and climbed up a railroad maintenance structure beside some train tracks. After I climbed down, I looked around and knew I was lost. I can always walk a long way it seems, but every time I make a choice it gambles to be the completely wrong one. I couldn't recognize anything. Every path I went down could have taken me anywhere in search for my backpack (which I had just walked off and left). I was stoned and getting worried I'd be wandering around lost all night again. I had never been to the main road proper and it was still so cloudy.

All the homes look so much the same. I thought I was going in circles, so I think I actually did. I really messed with what I could recognize. With only the strange echo of a highway bouncing off the buildings, I cut through gardens and random yards like a bat to get back to that pavilion. I was walking through a different entrance still not believing I was in the same park I'd left. Whew, my backpack was still there. The trees in this park look like the trees in every garden and in every temple…Alone, every sense of identity in me was shaken…I wrote myself to sleep.

# 35

The next day, the friends arrived and the breakfast they brought . . . *umai!* It had a cabbage and onion, green bean, and bell pepper delight in an olive oily delicatessen. The main course was on rice and the leftovers were on slices of bread. We smoked another joint, played frisbee, then went to the *onsen* sauna meditations. I gifted them my frisbee. After we were heated and cooled down, we puffed a cigarette, and bought some chocolate soft cream. We all departed from the *Supaa* market because everyone had to go to work.

As I was waiting for a ride rather uncomfortably, an angry old man on a bike rolled up. Staring at me across the intersection, not blinking an eye, as he crossed the road in a slow manner of caution. I was an animal he just wasn't sure about. His wide-rimmed *boshi* made him look like he was from an age past and I was his first sight of a new breed of humanity; a breed that sticks their left thumbs out at cars. He got closer and closer then stopped with his head leaning forward out of his neck trying to get a better look. He stared at me with a stolid almost offended look. I sort of laughed and he pedaled off…

Two of the most difficult words in English for the Japanese to distinguish between aurally is: work and walk. Hitchhiking was a bad taste in my mouth after all, so my feet started working in order to get stomped out. I started taking pictures of these crazy looking spider webs in a corner of some subway entrance stairwell and one of the three Japanese Jamaican friends that was a truck driver, honked his horn from behind me. There he and I were again! It was time to mount up. We conversed some more and after some kilometers, he let me out at an internet cafe in Naga-hama. I walked from Naga-hama to a small place past Omihachiman, called Yasu, where I curled up under a bridge for the night. The next day, I caught a ride from Yasu to Kyoto.

# *36*

▨▨▨ 7.5.08 ▨▨▨

## YOKING THE OX
## KYOTO, JAPAN

At the zen temple, Ryoan-ji, they had me take my shoes off before entering the building, but with all the chainsaws shattering the trees in the background, I had to believe the temple grounds still had everything the world brought with it. I'm not complaining. Ayumi-chan was a person I really felt comfortable with. She was intuitive and kind company who eased my expectation of those cultivated rock and sand garden trinkets. I meditated on the tiered deck overlooking the stone arrangement. It felt like I had to put a bubble around myself to feel the peace advertised. (Ayumi and I met through my host mother on the island of Hokkaido, and because I was staying with her mother in Kyoto for a few days, she flew down to see me around the city.)

The plant garden in Kyoto is a multicontinental plant extravaganza! My jaw dropped around every corner. The following day, we went for a hike in the hills surrounding Kyoto. We passed grandparent artists painting waterfalls and caught nearly invisible wood frogs. We took frequent mossy tree and chocolate breaks near the soft murmur from those innocent mountain creeks. I was spoiled with a smile, and I am forever grateful without a way to say it, "always bumbling for translation."

# *37*

## ShinKhanSen

Speed isn't something to be shunned.
Drill right through the mountain.
Spend bullets on bugs.
A broken cigarette and a flash of the world.
I'll die and remember nothing.
Fast forward.
Two broken cigarettes and the flash that the world is.
Neither above nor covert,
True Mind is on my windshield.
From the back of the train,
I hear it SPLAT.

While walking towards Ono-michi, the evening had come. When a man stopped to inquire if I needed an umbrella, "Present for you," he said and asked where I was from. I replied whimsically, "London." We drove back to his flat pad and drank a vending machine beer.

Our conversation was about his wife and how angry at him she was. He had to live in a small lonely house where he often fantasized about younger women. He smoked three packs a day, and boy, could he smoke! British accented Japanese is a funny one to try. It did strain, so Tomi taught me a neutral prayer: *"Nan Myou Hou Ren Gei Kyou"*

———

The next day, I rented a bike with the help of three-pack-a-day Tomi. I pedaled across to the southern chaos of small islands north of Shikoku without my backpack, because like a good fox, I can make a cache'.

To be honest, most of my bike ride was primarily along the street. The beauty of the islands struck me, but it always felt tainted by that ever-present crowd of humanity. I reached 'edge of the day' rather quickly due to a late start on the afternoon. I was on a bridge heading towards the island of Shikoku. As I travelled towards Japan's version of Maui on a very long and elaborate bridge. The sun began to set, and my vantage point was wanting so I picked up my pace on the bicycle to get the best view of what was to happen next. We are all familiar, I hope, with the thing I would describe. Can it be said in such a word? Sunset? It seems to be a mundane experience to us so much of the time, until you chase after one.

The aftermath of yesterday's heat coupled with today's exposure has reddened my arms and legs to the delirious color of an over-ripened fruit. Please don't touch me for surely, I would turn painfully white again...It's all in temporal fun and the chronic questioning, nibbling from the globe's theologies; always trying to understand through the push and pull of an animal's magnetics. After all my wine was finished, the moon reflected harvest red like a vertical pupil of a snake that slivered down into the southern waters of Japan.

That night, I dipped into an even more glorious phosphorescent phenomenon. I stirred up the water by the strongest wing beats my arms could conjure on that other side. All the while, one of my feet was being bitten by something unknown from out of the depths. For real this time.

*1*

The answer to my "riddle" goes like this: In order to lift something, the object must be moved away from a point of reference—in this case a gravitational center. "Can an omnipotent God create a rock so heavy, He can't lift it?" If one were to make something infinitely heavy, it would become so heavy that it would actually *become* that center in space.

If this object was to become so heavy that space could no longer hold it up, it would then collapse upon itself and create a black hole. The object would no longer exist. The answer is: "If God created such a rock, it would cease to be."

To be completely honest, I am deeply frustrated. Plants sit on their pedestals soaking up the sun and the animals creep around with qualities growing right out of their very bodies. Whatever that resource is in me is consumed by an overactive child's mind! By the time most animals, human size, are two years old, it has its seasons figured out or it dies. I'm sitting here alive and lost as the driftwood. I hang but not well hung. No wonder men became robbers and thieves with such a disadvantage. We are too erect to be actual monk-eys and all are too weak to be true to guerilla. The animals wander around with their three stomachs eating the raw leaves with nothing other than mastication for preparation. I can't step quietly in this modern society, let alone out of it, without an endless tool belt. "Why did I not grow the very thing that would ensure my feral opportunity!?"

In Greek mythology, when the titans were distributing the qualities among the various creatures, by the time they got to man, they had run out. So, Prometheus stole fire from an Olympian god to give it to a man, I don't know. Prometheus was henceforth punished for his action. He was tied to a rock and eternally eaten on by an eagle, day after undying day…

If the control over fire *truly* was our gift, it would not have been born of such a hindrance to our eternal selves; flames would spark pleasingly out of our fingertips, but instead, it burns us as much as the next combustible material. Manipulated and carefully smoking, this whole world wide is designing to be bitten off and chewed by fire: chewed off but not consumed. Like a carnivorous bird with a dysfunctional tongue, fire is always tearing and flicking but never swallowing. As are those insatiable qualities pretending to be "enjoying the meal." These black holes of our mouths will never be satisfied until all the fires are swallowed up by the exploding sun! Some of the animals have time. I am not so sure about me. Prometheus stole from the phoenix. It seems that his body was regenerated like fertilizer over all the Earth because his story seems to be everywhere. We can only hope to clean this up and add the right kinds of bodies to our flames of desire…

# *38*

## 7/8 Time

In the land of Samurai, I am allowed to write my own *seppu-ku*…aka suicide by cutting my stomach open and having my friend chop off my head onto a white cloth.

This Father Paul offered me a ride and I turned it down. I'll drink from his holy water but it wasn't he who blessed it. He offered me ease and a quick ride, but I was seeing in a distant island that I could swim across the expanse of water that was before me, without whoever he was. He wouldn't be coming with me anyways. The island beckoned and I jumped in.

*Swi swi swi.* It started off well, yet trying to breathe from little waves that splash over your face without a set of aqualungs, started killing me. Saltwater burns the throat and disorients the mind. It scares the breath away. I started to feel weak. The distance had a current to fight, and I got carried diagonally through my projected route…I was fighting to inhale through that disorientation, I was swallowing and then coughing back up. I had to lay back and back-stroke to stare up at the sky. Thoughts swirled through my head, "I am swallowing too much salt water," "I am a terrible swimmer," "It is still so far away," "My head sure feels funny." I had left my backpack back on the shore at least, but it was a battle enough to stave off fear. When no one can save you from the dead end that is before you, one starts to wonder, "What is in a wonder-ball?" Ribbit. I got to the island pumped and skeptical if I could swim back. "Its high tide and I am on the driest beach I have ever known." I rested for a minute and collected seashells from the sand near my feet. I found blue heron feathers and started feeling better. I decided to swim back with the mindfulness of presence this time around.

That current that I had fought seemingly dropped me off back on the shoreline. For a peace of mind, I had to triple-take to reassure myself of the distance and strange feelings I had just experienced. While I was in the water, I had told myself, "This isn't the end!" It was an anticlimactic sizzle, and I rebelled against it. The seppu-ku wasn't there. For anyone willing to go where there is nothing: no man or medicine to come and rescue. . . my thought is: don't bait yourself out there with promises of reward, only prayers.

# 39

Blisters on Blisters on blisters . . . I've been walking for three days now and I've got one more 28 killme trek until I reach Hiroshima. My toes look like hamburger. Hitchhiking and writing signs worked only so well. I would get dropped off as soon as the mouth of a city was met. I would then have to walk the pavement until I found an exit ramp on the other side of whatever specific city I was dropped at. I didn't even try standing in the sun or rain with my thumb out until I was more confident that there weren't just intramural travelers.

It felt like I was walking so much anyways, I committed to it.

All along this way, I saw the *Obaa-chan*. She is the great grandmother. She is usually the sweetest but has her days. Daily, they work to take care of the children and grandchildren as well as tend and hand plant the rice and vegetable gardens. After cooking and consoling their husbands, her wrinkled smile is a photograph of relentless experience. I like to picture them with their curved over spines, hunched beneath conical wicker hats; wearing a red and blue flower blouse, patiently tending the hardy staffs of life, and every so often, she looks up and sees that, by those labors, her family survives well into the winters of father time.

I slept that night like a city bum in Kure-shi Park with no one else to kiss me goodnight except the mosquitoes. I looked down and just kept walking. (Kilometers later . . .)

I'm stepping out of memory. If I walked for the eternity, my mind would empty. Overwhelmed like a child seeing the world for the first time, I scream and tear like the shock treatment of being born. I am not apart from this world, but I appear nameless within my own body. What am I? There is that sadness of the heart like death, the sadness of everything smiling while they die. I am attached to the beautiful, but I have only two eyes and I hate wanting. When it's this hot, all I really want is ice cream. So, I scream @

# 40

# 広島市

HIROSHIMA

Hiroshima isn't an island as far as I can tell…I had been sleeping in the Peace Park for a few days on the staircase that steps down to the river. While sitting on that side of the river in Hiroshima the flute I had with me was keeping me company. Sound and sequence problem can ease your mind (even when you aren't very good at it.)

I had refused to participate in the pictorial horrors of the World War II monument. *Genbaku* Dome's skeleton was my backdrop and shadow enough. I don't know… The thought of humans being bleached alive didn't seem like something I really wanted to see. Hiroshima-shi is the city to actually symbolize a world's peace born from a nuclear retaliation. That very bomb is said to be what brought Japan's emperor from out of his high castle. Listening to this girl talk the other night, I learned Japan, as a country, refuses to arm itself with nuclear weapons. Tidal policies on explosives might be changing due to the times.

After one week in Hiroshima, I was feeling very self-conscious about a party I had missed. I was invited by a pretty girl…Not a good premise. I tortured myself until nightfall the next day. Unable to make the move, I was somehow rescued by musicians I found beneath the Peace Park bridge. They welcomed me inn.

The band beneath the bridge, consisted of a group of two other man-cubs and a she-cub. They busked the strips where all the commerce is trafficked for tips and experience. Caught up in the moment, I forgot about the girl with the party and the band there became my only experience.

Hiroshi-kun was a guitar player but he kept the rhythm on the box drum from Brazil. I doodled on his box drum called *el cajon* with Hiroshi-kun on his guitar. He was a philosopher and knew my same trick for buying beer under the age.

I couldn't go anywhere in Japan without drawing some attention from the Japanese, so when another set of eyes started hanging out listening, I didn't think too much of it.

I started talking with him some but it took a moment for his story to sink into me. Hiroshi-kun and I were going to go get some *okonomi-yaki* for dinner at a place he knew well, but this Naotaka, we just met, wanted to meet up with us afterwards. He couldn't join us for dinner because he was using his paper sparingly. His metaphor was not to take too much from the toilet paper roll every time he had to wipe his butt….

"Both in heaven and hell, delicious food exists. The people there all eat with very long chopsticks. The only difference between the two is that in heaven, your neighbor brings the food to your mouth, while in hell, everyone just tries to feed themselves." -Hiroshi-kun

"*Itadakimasu!*" After din-din say, *"Gochisosama deshita,"* I sorta failed to buy Naotaka dinner…Later though, we managed to all meet up again. Hanging out, another girl joined up with us and we sat and listened to the band, jam their sets in the enclosed shopping district.

The band couldn't stay too late and most likely went home to their families, but we didn't have any. I convinced Naotaka that we should make the evening into a night and loosen the roll, because how did the Indians do it? (With plants of course!) We bought some beer and dessert like good braves and passed them around. We met another even younger kid and the five of us spread out some bedding to fall asleep like the gypsy van in the imaginary Peace Park.

# 41

The next morning, we all got up and sorted through our things. Saying farewell together, Naotaka and I parted ways with Hiroshima and her friends in the early afternoon.

I had left America with my father's blessing, but Naotaka had left his home rather violently. He owned a van and everything he owned was in that van. He renounced his family's name and asked me to call him Kozaku. "Aizaku" and "Kozaku". He was looking for a new scene and adapted to my mission to get to a hotel south of Fukuoka. We had a little under a week to get to Nankan and there wasn't a spare seat, so I squished into the side of his van like a piece of luggage.

I learned that Naotaka was nineteen. My birthday was less than two months away and I had started to tell people I was already twenty due to its proximity and "legality." When Naotaka asked my age in Hiroshima, I answered him from that pattern of thought. It wasn't till later when we were bathing in the *onsen* together that I corrected it to the truth.

In order to get from the mainland of Honshu to the island of Kyushu there has been constructed an underwater tunnel that connects the two island's roadways. We split the toll and crossed under, to get over. With the spirit of adventure and excitement, "Kozaku" whistled Steven Spielberg's Jurassic Park's theme song nearly perfectly and I playfully imitated George Lucas's Yoda.

I can only justify recounting this story because it was beautiful. We drove all through the day and into the night around Kyushu looking for a place to be. *Achi kochi, achi kochi.* For hours we didn't know what to do or where to go. Somehow in the middle of the night, we found the "spot".

I could write "niji no matsubara" but it wouldn't make any sense to anyone unfamiliar. I do apologize. I sometimes don't like reading books like these…The Rainbow's Pine Forest is what we found. More so, we woke up inside of it. I don't know how old that forest is but it has been cared for, for a long time. The trees are sixty-foot tall bonsai pine. It is right on the coast north of Nagasaki. The forest is miles long and very narrow following the beach into the city of Karatsu. I couldn't resist climbing up a few of those trees, they were too tempting.

We reached the luxurious hotel the English Camp teachers were meeting up in, north of Nankan. I'm very happy we went there, but I came away with a sense of regret. It became strange when I didn't get the chance to say goodbye to Kozaku. He left the next day on his own and I have never heard from him again. I imagined that he had to go back to his family to procure a passport because in the Shinto tradition, the last name is always introduced first.

# 42

## ENGLISH CAMP

After our potty breaks, we got snacks. The kindergarteners peeled and threw the biggest grapes I've ever seen at me, then playfully climbed both my legs like koala bears. I've never met a barrel of koala bears that like peanut-butter and jelly more than those Japanese-lings. I am happy I am not made of sturdier stockings, because I get to turn whatever age I have already been. We battled their rhinoceros beetles and fed the rice-paddy spiders, grasshoppers, instead of worrying about mass extinction.

# *43*

## "Once upon a time in Tokyo"

After the English lessons came to an end, I flew from Fukuoka City to Tokyo. My Japanese teacher's son, Susumu, met me at the train station outside of Haneda airport. We knew we were like brothers almost immediately seeing as how I had just been learning from his mother like a child.

We went out that night and he introduced me to his girl-friend, Aichan. The first thing that she said aloud was, *"Kao ga chichai ne,"* not knowing I would understand. She said, "His face is small isn't it," I'm sure she felt pretty embarrassed, but I just agreed with her.

The next night, Susumu-kun, Ai-chan, her friend Minami-chan and I all went out for *sashimi, sake,* and smoke at an *Izakaya* Bar. After being seated, I got to meet the girl across from me. I liked the way *she* smoked. I liked the way she looked at me. I liked how she told the story of John Lennon meeting Yoko Ono. I held her hand as we left.

"In the art gallery, climb up the ladder-stairs to a little peephole. Peeking through, awaiting, is a word, 'yes'."

We walked around Shibu-ya in downtown Tokyo, but the city's lights couldn't dazzle me in my happy-hour *karaoke* song. (Karaoke is much different in Japan. It is more personal like a private party. The group rents out a room and can order food or drinks to accompany the sing-along.)

We went for the *nomihodai*—all you can drink. I wasn't afraid of trying but I don't think that I impressed her with my voice. Her name meant "South" but I was heading back East the next day. I met her homebound train, yet we were going in perpendicular directions…On the platform, entirely surrounded by strangers, her body felt so warm to me. I could have been a specter raised up from the concrete crypt. Saying goodbye, we held each other and kissed like a long-lost prayer, chanted, but never knowing its translation. With the help of little queens that like to share in secret notes, I am becoming a better use to my back pockets. She wrote it, and I held it, but I never took her breath away. The next day, I boarded a plane and flew back to the United States of America.

# 44

 8.15.08

## HUMBOLT STATE UNIVERSITY

About a week after returning from Japan, I moved to Arcata, California. I respectively spent two semesters studying Botany, Anthropology and Yoga. I felt challenged to make the most of my time on this planet. There has been an echo of that whispered, "take it" in my brain for so long, I was haunted, ever since the City of Rocks trip a few years ago.

"How could such a whispering exist and what does it mean?"

The question certainly begets an uncouth connotation when so closely associated with psychedelics. I was actually on my own in a world I never manifested.

## 12.6.08

*I'm the type of guy who likes water with his wine. For obvious promptings and a deep unsettlement, I began my purification fast. End of day 1 and I feel better already. My thoughts have already been cleared of the cloud that was thickest, called uncertainty. Mental acuity can be a prized possession and for a very long time I have abused it without any maintenance. I have called in the plumber and he is here to flush the pipes. I crossed my middle and forefingers for blessings over a continuous ten days of water and cayenne pepper in the middle of final's week.*

## 12.10.08

*I feel fine when I am sitting down in thought thinking. It's when I try to get up and do things that I really notice how fatigued I feel. I am drinking water and one sixteen-ounce mixture of lemon juice,*

*cayenne, and two tablespoons of maple syrup a day.*

## 12.13.08

*I can't walk thirty yards without getting lightheaded. I don't want to overplay this but I feel like I am dying. I sense a depression deep in my bones, but I have never felt so connected to my core. I notice my body has the ability of a concert. Where I was split in two, from the solar plexus down, I am now one.*

## 12.15.08

*Something isn't right. I can't keep this up. I've lost twelve pounds and I was never overweight. I'm calling it: nine and a half days. I didn't feel like it was a fold but I did watch my cards and my chips disappear. Dates and pecans eaten together . . . I have nothing to say except, "high on life."*

# 1.23.09

*I went back to Arcata after Christmas with intentions to fully listen to that inner voice that nudges me in specific directions, only to realize through retrospect that they were the "right" ones. It reveals a pit fall when I don't pay heed. The whispering isn't always reliable like something that refuses to be all that there is to the experience of the ego. So far, from the best I can make of it, I am subscribing it to, "The Voice of Seeing" from Carlos Castenada's coin or a.k.a, Jiminy Cricket.*

Because I found Matsu.

Matsu-chan, like *Raksha,* is my wolfmother. She is a half-breed, German Shepherd/wolf-dog named after that empty castle in Matsumoto, Japan. Listening to that voice, I found her six weeks after her birth in Blue Lake, CA between Redding and Arcata. At my first sight of her lagging behind her other siblings, I felt that subtle *somethingness* in the moment. I tried to talk her breeder down in price, but he said to me, "This is going to be a good dog. If you don't buy her, I am going to keep her." I paid him $200 of my roommate's rent money, picked her up and brought her to my A-frame haven off Janes Road. I told my father I was short on rent that month... Karmically, it was primarily her and I throughout the unaccountable times of this book. I was like any man-made coherent through the devotion, to his family of animals.

*45*

 6.1.09

BOISE, IDAHO

I've never told anyone about all that happened in Arcata, but here is a snapshot of what it was like the morning before I left.

I didn't sleep.

I had soaked a bag of pinto beans in water until they were swollen and their *prana* was bright. Tip-toeing around the sleeping bags containing my friends from Idaho, I took a Q-tip and went to all the black widow spider webs in my house and twirled them up. I started a fire and recycled much of my clothes and school papers in the wood stove. The sun was just breaking to the east and Matsu was still sleeping. I put the pinto beans into a container, brought them outside and sowed them in a full circle around the A-frame. When I looked up, the morning mist was disappearing in the heat of a new day.

If anyone has ever tried to watch a plant grow in real time before, they would know how tedious it is. They are alive in a different time signature than us. That morning, the plants awoke in a phenomenon I have never heard of before. If I have ever drawn an honest breath, the hostas in my back yard, on a windless day were drawing their leaves up and down in a movement that spanned at least six inches—over and over, up and down, up and down, until I looked away...

Matsu and I moved to Boise together with some old friends. One of my wolfbrothers was heading towards Pocatello soon to visit his family. I was fresh out of Arcata and I wasn't ready to jump into new cycles without clearing my space from all that space. I asked my friend if he would drop me off in the City of Rocks on his way to Pocatello.

At the CTR turn into the City of the Rocks in Almo, I stepped out of his car. It had rained recently and the dark brown of the sage stems said, "We drink through our bark as well." The meadowlarks echoed each other from across the blanket of sage brushes, soothing.

Matsu and I had gathered ourselves together on another period of transition without any of the usual party responsibilities. Before my wolfbrother left, we confirmed we had plans for our pack to meet up in the City in a week from then. I was in no hurry. I set my camp up backcountry where the living water leisurely flows down from.

# 46

While hiking through a ravine, Matsu ran up ahead of me and out of ear shot. I looked up the hillside to the right of me and perched on a fencepost, was a large bird…I double backed. Crouching in reverse, climbing up behind a tall rock to the blindside of the bird, I peered around a scraggly notch and pulled out my binoculars. I couldn't believe it. It was a gyrfalcon. The gyrfalcon is an arctic bird that only migrates to southern latitudes during the fall or winter. Here it was just out of breeding season! I got twenty yards before that white bird of prey jumped and swooped down behind the neighboring cliffs; the largest falcon in the *world*. Here comes Matsu storming down the trail!

Two days later Matsu and I were hiking up the hill to the spines of that stegosaur. There is this crescent bowl in them that I love to sit in the evenings. Most days it's just deer and the approaching starlight to enjoy, but this time it was serious. Matsu was in lead and she kicked a fallen limb of a juniper. Uproarously, the telltale sign of a rattler sounded off, *"Chotto matte!"*

"Matsu! *Tomare!"* That inner voice kicked in, "You know what to do." It took its defensive stance and sideslithered around itself. Their coil is a steel-spring snap I wasn't about to stick my hand into. Donovan rang in my ear, "Rikki-Tikki-Tavi mongoose is gone." I picked up a stick and compressed its head to the ground. I reached down and grabbed its body at the beginning of its neck. The jaws opened and flailed from side to side to scrape its fangs into my lymph. The body reeled like an eel out of water. I started squeezing. I could feel the snake's aura creeping up my arm and it became my duty to fight it out. The mouth closed and we stared into each other's eyes. They were an olive green with striations of red around the vertical pupil. Its rattle never ceasing, the snake started winning the arm wrestle. My right hand alone began to feel drained up to the forearm. I cinched down my grip with my left. The connection that both of my hands made completed the circuit and the rattlesnake's vital energy had nothing to gain. The color of the sensation changed to blue and I absorbed it into my own.

I put the live snake on the ground and watched it. I would have let it go, but it had no more luck. I followed each step of our carnivorous natures and learned from it. I love rattlesnakes in all their delicate and deadly beauty. The only reason I interfered with this one is because I had a lucid dream the week before, that I would be encountering one. I believed it when I saw it. My inner voice clarified that this was the one. If I left it the way it was, it would have not been right. I took the stick and finished it off. I chopped its head off and placed it on a stone. I cut it open and swallowed its heart. By this time, my body was in shivers and I started a fire and heated a different stone on the coals until the snake was cooked. Matsu and I ate her. I buried the head, gifted the skin, and returned the rattle to the lairs where they dwell.

# 47

After all that, I still had three days before my brothers would show up. I had with me *theobroma cacao* beans, yerba mate, and grapefruit juice. I had no real date to go by, so I started fasting in hope to be in-tune with their arrival. They do have a presence like that. Three days I was. The body began to get into a rhythm with the weather. The rains were daily but every morning, the sun would be up long enough to dry out my night's moisture from the bivouac and sleeping bag. In the evening, the clouds would return. Every day it rained except the third. It was a day of all sun and appropriately the day they were going to show up. I waited exclusively for them but they never arrived…Breaking my fast with some oyster mushrooms I had gathered, I continued to dodge the rain from there.

## "Ode in the City"

Clapping wings
Chrysalis sun panels
Yellow disc flowers
Mule's ear, thunder shower
A prayer pose
*Kaminari!*
I haven't eaten a valkyrie yet today.
It is what the cats have always had to do.
overcast green and blurry blue
drupelets roll down the waxy vein
these leaves are turgid after a rain
superficial grey and wet brown
dirt clods cling to my dampened feet
deep moon craters dimple from the sleet
purple lupine and olivine sage
my mothers beg for all I am willing to eat
Her eyes leak love like a wolf.
lacquered sand and bleached bone
naked animal sheds like
chiseled stone
Death is as vibrant as Life
Death is as vibrant as Life
Rumi was a Sufi.
Slowly, I look inward then outward . . .
For *mi amor*
that hidden desert,
compass Rose.


—*Mowgli, Storm-Dodger*

The rains came early one afternoon while my gear was out drying. I was away on a hike. Nine days and twenty pounds of water weight heavier, I rolled my gear into my backpack. It was evidently time to go. Heading towards Elba, I had no time for dejection, though, not with Matsu, moon and me, *squish squish squish,* after each step.

# INTERMISSION . . .

*48*

## PSYCHOLOGY, POLITICS, AND
## COSMOLOGY *WITHOUT* CONCLUSION

What's a walkabout without its take on spirituality? I like the walkabout that makes sense in the end. To me, it all ties back together, but my issue has always been communicating it.

If anyone started talking about religion around my grandfather, he would bend over and start rolling up his pant legs. If you asked him what he was doing he would say, "I don't want to get shit on my pants while wading through this bull." I recommend that we all roll up our pant legs at this time.

# 49

## "Psalms 6/8"

When the Church is your wife, what kind of censoring
goes on inside of your mind?

It is the Foreshadow . . .

The Muse says, "It is time."
Moses steps out of the mountains
Ten Commandments close in hand.
He tells his people to murder the idolaters.
Still they wed and reproduced, mixed population
and mixed signals
because The I Am has split all the damned songs in
halves.

Then he puts them back together again,
double-time just to say that he can.
Chaos.
Conscious Chaos
Artful Chaos


Humpety-Dumpety.


Germany's philosopher said, "God is dead, we have killed
him."


Frederich Neitzsche ate too much from the accursed
comedy.
Parents playing the same tricks on their own children. . .


Sonar has bled the brains
Of they, who are submersible.
No one likes the taste of their own medicine.


As in Jacob dreaming the Stairway,
Astraea was given the scales
and the very doG carries the tick marks


Rule of the thumbed.


Admit to textual lacuna!
*Mene, Mene, Tekel, Parsin*


God has decided
To date and go out with the Whales.
"God is dead, we have killed him."

Ten-lined June-beetle 19th, 2013:
We will have only these 7 years . . .
To save the damned yet favored whales!
Why *can't* we hear the footfall of the Almighty? Job 41:1

He can have very slippery flippers (when he chooses.)
Does anyone understand
from a zookeeper's interpretation for the multitudes?

The Temple of Heaven *is* within!
Let the brother's Dome on the Rock STAY!
Truly love thy "Enemy," and leave this Abominable
House of Hypocritters.

The Messianic Age has been 2400 years in waiting . . .
If there is yet to be a Messiah
He already exists.
If the Messiah has already been
He still exists.
As is the nature of the timelessness.
Personally, I haven't raised the serpent from the depths
and given it four legs.
It has done that upon her own acchord-ion.
"Check yo Mate"
"Be not afraid, O land; be glad and rejoice . . . Be not
afraid, O wild animals . . ." Joel 2:21

.". . Your sons and daughters will prophesy . . . your
young men will see visions." Joel 2:28
— *JaH's WeH*

If the entire world *was* created by a being, beyond the fourth dimension of time, then take all the variables of Time out of the equations. Calculus assumes with every derivative that infinity goes to Zero, which is the fallacy. Infinity goes to infinity. They accept it, so that they can move on, mathematically. I cannot. The world stops spinning for something like that.

I am not a man of lawlessness. I am a man-cub of Natural Law, and this 6/8 Dream is not so fat, so fun, little track. It isn't uncomfortable to bathe nude with complete strangers in the Japanese-sense unless the "stranger" is hiding from one's own-self and in this particular passage, from extinction.

# *50*

## "Did you roll your pant legs up?"

The Bible's meanings have been written very cryptically right from the beginning, especially the words of Jesus. Luke 17:37 NIV: "Where Lord?, they asked. He replied, '*Where there is a dead body, there the vultures will gather'.*" This is the verse that I am building my argument from. I have looked at three different versions, as well as Chuck Swindoll's *Insights on Luke.* The Greek translates directly to "eagle". The King James Version reads "eagle", but the New International Version reads "vulture". I have used the symbolism of the vulture within my own writing as something with a dis-eased nature. I recommend Chuck Swindoll because he goes the next step to say that the bird named is one of prey with an evil nature and makes a paraphrase in reference to Job 39:26-30 which reads very clearly that the hawk eats meat, which he can see from afar…Everything is as clear as mud.

The Greek text most directly says eagle with nothing surely mentioned about a *dead* body. "We're talking about the coming of the kingdom of God." *"Two will be grinding grain; one is left."* The way the NIV version reads is as if fifty percent of the world's population dies and gets eaten by evil vultures. Reading the others make hints at something more like the mounting up on the wings of eagles. *Trans*literation? Even if it should read "vulture" there is nothing "evil" about a carrion bird eating carrion. Animals do die. My own symbolism refers to the carrion bird trying to eat something that isn't dead yet. "Look alive!" It is true that after a battle, eagles would come from afar and eat the fallen. I am saying that this nature isn't "evil". I would like to bring attention to Revelation 19:17-21 "if we all have our Bibles open at this time." The angel mentioned in that passage, actually *summons* birds to eat the dead…

There comes a time when we need to step out of the parable-poetic-speak and just say what's needed to be said. The ten-lined June beetle is an insect from the mountains I live in. I believe that June 19th, 2020 will be an event-horizon; I'm not sure yet what kind…

# 51

WHAT I AM ABOUT TO TELL YOU FEELS LIKE A
DIRTY LITTLE SECRET.

The importance of a name is believed to have everlasting consequence. I agree that, how we address each other and how we address Consciousness, itself, is of great importance. It has the ability to either unite or fragment our own thinking. Monotheism is well understood to be in continual conflict over the One-True name of God. The word "Allah" is nothing more than the Arabic word for God. Yet being, the Anglo-Saxon that I am, I would never adopt "Allah" as my native name for God, unless I was very specifically addressing the god of Islam from the Koran.

This big BUTT lies in how we have accepted that in English, the Christian God, just needs a capital letter. Lowercase "god" is everything but the Christian one. The kicker is…The word "God" has Germanic origins: *Gott* or *Guda*. Truthfully speaking, there is no *Gudan* in the Bible. I'll say this another way, "There is no God in the Bible." Technically, we all have been praying to a historically alive and real German deity (based upon basic rules of translation). Most Muslims know this intrinsically and refuse to allow the Koran (or even the name "Allah") to be translated. The Bible teaches that "God the Father" goes by many names. None of which are physically pronounced, "Gawd," because, quite frankly, it isn't in the ancient texts of the Bible. Furthermore, the Holy Tetragram, that is the unspeakable name, revered as transcendent of language, has been taken out of the English Versions. Why would that be? Not a single name of "YHWH" from the Hebrew and Greek texts, that make up the Bible, has gone unadulterated in the entire course of the Christian Church. (Latin isn't in the Bible either.) We don't really know who is listening when we say a generic term like Gawd. He is an idea alienated from its native land. If "God" is native to all lands then so is Allah, Brahma, Zeus, and so on.

I am tempted to go through all the Bible and whenever it has the word "God", replace it with "Allah" just to make my point. Is it really that difficult to learn a few words to be certain that you are addressing the Biblical Deity? (i.e. *Elohim)* or have you been stripped of that power?

*"Well, we still have Jesus!"*

Who *is* Jesus? The books Matthew, Mark, Luke, and John are known as the Gospels. Gospel means "the good news". "Christ," according to Webster's Ninth Colligate

Dictionary, may also be defined to mean an, "ideal form of humanity." Usually, "Christ" means "Savior" or "Messiah", one in the same. The story of Joseph and Mary giving birth to a child is found at the beginning of each gospel.

Nazareth is where Lesou is from: Lesou [yay-su] of Nazareth. Nazareth was an occupied country in the fertile crescent of the Mediterranean…We can delineate from history that everything boiled down to the two feuding brothers, Romulus and Remus. After killing his brother for the empire, Rome had in place an overlord to rule the locals, named Pilot. The Jewish nation had kept its sovereignty only in its religious practices, following the laws of Moses. When Lesous was 32, he claimed presence in the Jewish nation as fulfillment of prophesy from Isaiah and like Socrates they adhered to his blasphemy, with that which corrupts the youth. He claimed to be the Son of God (or of YHWH?). Curiously, Lesou *also* claimed to be the "Son of Man". His mother had no intercourse to bring him into the world. Rather, he had been born into the world, half-man, half-god!

Who is Hercules again? How would you feel as a Roman, after praying to dead, demigods your entire life, to hear of a real one from the northeast? Christianity spread like it wasn't just meant to be. Instead of a war-faring and violent warrior, they got the healer. As the Roman Empire collapsed, factions of Catholicism tied the land back together with a very tight knot.

As I understand it, YSH (Hebrew) or Lesous (Greek) means, "YHWH's Helper". That's what the name "Jesus" is trying to mean. Why isn't that common knowledge and being taught?

Lingo spends like tobacco when there is more than one spiritual group, yet if gathered together, whittle strictly to the point. Before we armored ourselves against the other, the "gauntlet" was known as a falconer's glove. This present gauntlet now comes at the end of every journey. It has become the passage through hell from one paradise to another . . . "running the gauntlet" as in a baby being born and then eventually forgetting about it.

I find myself both a creator and an object of creation, yet in a world of entropy (where everything seeks the path of least resistance) ghosts are more available than adults. Observing, that it is well within our power to either breed or destroy our very tribe, I have had no absolute teaching to swear loyalty to. It wasn't until after, I divided from my family and their tradition did my own creativity seek to climb the steepest grade. Sport climbing rocks and mountains has become a life and death matter of the overly selfconscious revival! In Buddhism, the Bhodisattva that walks directly to the gates of transcendence is almost always turned back, driven outward and onward 'till reunited with the greatest family he or she can possibly justify knowing.

Ever since I reconsidered my own name from birth, the Bible has become an interesting ally. Lesou is already a perfect example like an unannounced zen master to openly end animal sacrificing in a single stroke. It has been dissonant to neglect learning from our brothers and their hoods from then on. That was 2,013 years ago. Without the master around, what are we going to do about it? I have been told from the moment of my incarnation that I cannot become Him. I may only become like Him. Although, the person they did name me to become wasn't someone they considered, spoken from the mouth of an unsanctioned river. If I wanted to, I could be diligent enough to make zero connections and keep my life in its own and individual existential box, training in the candid observation that has no thoughts or opinions of its causality. However, I admire what happens when the lines of intricacies overlap in such a dense web that it forms an entire picture. I may have taken this too far, but I have a birth certificate saying, I am Isaac.

> Give a man a fish,
> And he will eat for a day.
> Teach a man to fish,
> And he will build an empire of tools
> as West Nile vamps all the Oceans.

Isaac, son of Abraham B.C. is the younger brother ripped from his half-brother, Ishmael, then lain on an altar and surrendered up as a sacrificial offering. Biblically, the tribe of Israel could not have two sons from different mothers, both first-born to opposite women, squabbling over authority on down through the generations.

Chronologically, Isaac should have gotten the knife. As Abraham lifted up his arm, YHWH stayed him with the angelic blessing of a bleating ram. The brilliant remedy to the situation was to exile Ishmael and his mother to the harsh element, cremate the ram, and act as if nothing happened.

All brothers fight it out, but they hadn't finished growing together before that exile. The ancients weren't "weened" at the same time "we" are. Isaac wasn't a babe and would have remembered. When one is almost killed by their tribal leader yet saved in a last-minute decision of celestial favoritism; the laws of first-born heritage were broken, before they were created, and the elder, Ishmael, nearly abandoned by his defeated mother and embittered without his father, went into the desert to father the sons of Islam. To the Jews, he was remembered as a "wild ass of a man." (Genesis 16:12)

Years prior, Abraham was known as Abram. Upon the revelation of a son being born to Abram and his barren wife, Sarai, YHWH asked for a cow, a goat, and a sheep to be cut in half bilaterally and posed opposite to each other on the ground. The offerings of a dove and a pigeon were left intact, but when the birds of prey came down to eat, Abram drove them away. (Genesis 15: 9-11).

# 52

 3.15.12

It was a rainy winter's day in the City of Rocks National Reserve, and the snow was still lingering on the ground. My father helped me hike in some of my gear before we prayed for our survival and a toast from his sacrament. He reversed his SUV and steered away. It was just Jesus, Matsu-chani, and I then. I had a heart-appointment with the City, so I packed every belonging I would need to survive in this world. Fold or all-in. I had a skeleton of a plan but I had to muster up some muscle in order to carry it to and up into my cave. I had no clue how long I would be able to stay, so I prepared for an experience that had no end.

I got snowed in multiple times with soggy, soled boots resorting to stockpiling sage brush to burn and melt frigid powder for my water. I waited.

The days weren't exactly painful. With the sounds of my native-style flute ricocheting back and forth across the expanses, I had such a theatrical position. I was perched some 25 feet above the ground at the mouth of a cave of cliff swallows in the heart of Cities among inhuman cities. I bathed in the creeks on intermittent cloudless days and sought out the songs of birds I couldn't recognize. I discovered the Western Towhee.

# 53

When it comes to it, the ledge I'm feeling is that approach to where the reserves run out. It's the place where the acutely dazzling things happen, and when the days aren't counted. I was pinned under a tarp, waiting for a twelve-hour long storm to pass. With my wolf-matriarch and I huddled together, my mother's anxiety began to wash over me. I thought to myself, "Oh god, she's going to call in the coast guard on this land-locked state of mine, I just know it." I love my mama dearly and since I had arrived, I hadn't turned my cell phone on to talk to anyone. There was a narrow band of blue on the horizon and as I watched it approach, so did the next storm's front follow closely behind. I have seen enough motherly figures with separation anxiety, so I jumped up when that opportunity of blue came above me. I followed it for about an hour to where I could send and receive from distant space stations the news of my wellbeing. My younger sister answered, the call made on her birthday: March 26.

"Is Jeremy there yet?"

*"Que?"*

"Ya, he is on his way.

Actually, he should have gotten there already."

"What!?"

Ten years prior, my older brother by two years, became an apprentice to a falconer. He attained his own falconer license appropriately, but his red-tailed hawk died after training and my brother nearly followed suit from a deadly heart-palpitation caused by the over-consumption of Datura seeds. He was separated by hundreds of miles after that for years. I was 23 and he used to be my "best" friend. He knew where I was, generally speaking, but I had no idea where he was tracking to. Walking down that road to Almo, if I had been just fifteen minutes earlier, I would have intersected him perfectly after 12 days of not speaking to anyone. Instead, we both met up with our dogs back at my cave. We spent an entire week together through the sleet turning to rain outside his tent. His presence couldn't have been more welcomed. I had been watching a pair of kestrel falcons scrape their ledges for their upcoming hatchlings all that week. I had been wondering about my brother frequently, but it wasn't my first time in the City of Rocks and her lonely weather.

It had fallen to me to sort through what belongings everyone had left behind. More than curiously, I found my brother's two remaining red-tailed hawk's *jesses* in the City with me. I brought them only because they had made their way into my leather working kit. After an anklet is attached to a bird of prey's ankle, strips of leather are then threaded through the grommet until the "button" on the end meets the anklet. The two *jesses* are joined together with a *sampo* swivel. During our years apart it had been very difficult for me to relate to him. One night around that campfire, I asked him, "When are you going to get back into falconry?" We decided each of us would take one of the kangaroo leather *jesses* as a token for our futures together.

Before my brother left, my father came out to meet us with unanimous support. Beneath the Ram of Aries, my sister, Rachel, the female ewe, unsacrificed, met that future October 22, 2012; licenses in hand.

The biblical story of Isaac and Ishmael seems to me a pivotal turning-point in history. With five different animals sacrificed, Abram doesn't seem to take into account that he did so in such a way, that it stands above all other types of animal sacrificing. (Usually the animal is bled out and burnt.) Cutting an animal in half and facing it in opposition to itself, yet leaving a pigeon and dove intact, I interpret that as the only hope. It was to feed the raptors that would eventually bring the brothers back together.

If it is indeed possible to be reincarnated, even if only for just a piece of your story, then I would say, "As was Isaac B.C.'s *yoga.*"

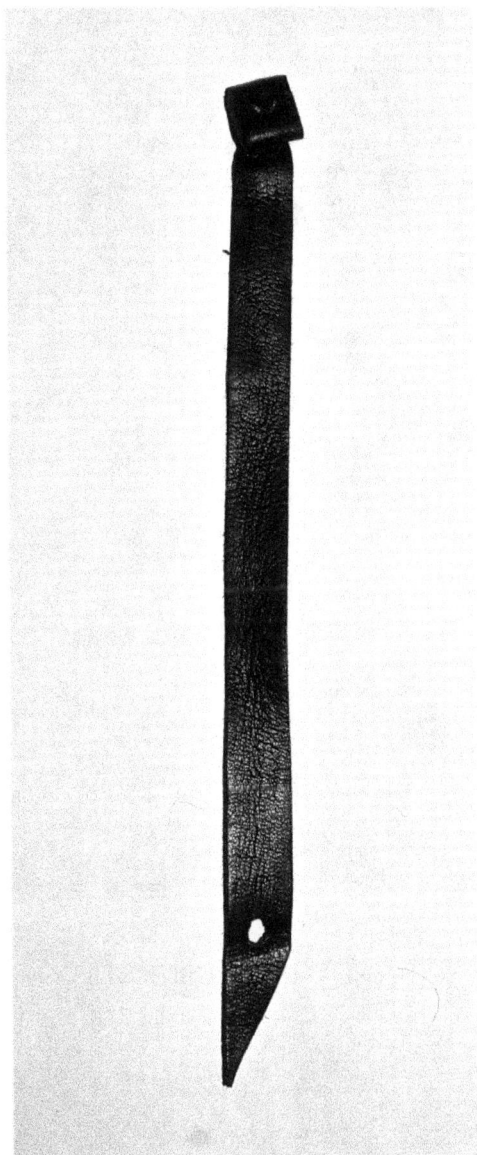

I NAMED HER, 'EUPHRATES".

# 54

## THE DREAM REALM OF THE 7TH SEAL
## CASCADE, IDAHO

After compiling on this book for an entire rotation around the sun, training hawks and searching for that Dream Woman dressed in red from my acid visions, I finally found her.

Within the perspective, there was something in front of me. I decided a few minutes ago to take a nap because all I wanted to do was sleep. After I closed my eyes, I wasn't seeing rest. I saw her.

I noticed a small scroll lodged in the left side of her abdomen. Naturally, I pulled it out and opened it. The scroll was undecorated like brass about eight inches long, unrolling for approximately three feet. I let it sway as if in a slight wind just before I tore it in half.

I saw a vision of my mother coming out of a hospital room and collapsing in tears at the knowledge of being pregnant with her third child, me. There was some type of channel to the sky from the crown of her head. A sparkle of light came down into her, then down into her womb.

When I saw this, the sutures in my skull relaxed and out of the top of my head, a light emerged. After I tore the scroll in half, another light emerged. I rolled up the scroll and threw it away into the dark. Looking up, I saw my light eaten first. Hers was soon after. The Cosmic Viper surrounding this planet ate them.

If ayahuasca is new to you, it is a Death Rattler. When the lights were both swallowed, this snake's rattle-tail burst from the inside out. From the stub grew two more desperate tails. The two tails curved towards each other and created a cliché heart, then formed a butterfly's silhouette. Immediately after, the serpent bit onto its metamorphic tail and began to consume itself to only its head. Once the heavens were empty, out of the Great Rift beneath the Atlantic Ocean arose an anaconda. It peaked its head out of the surface of the water and tasted the air.

In its own awareness of time it slithered through the water. It swam to the Kenyan coastline and beached. Front legs sprouted and it dragged its body onto land. The two spurs around the cloaca fully sprouted into its hind legs and this four-legged snake then transfigured into the form of an everglade's alligator. The Alligator crawled north and took watch over a True North Pole. Aurora expanded like a blue energy growing, encasing the entire planet.

The week I had this dream, there were two towers being built for a climbing competition. I had paid fifty-five dollars to participate in it. The day after that serpentine dream (on the day of the competition), I woke up with President Obama in my mind's eye. He was contemplatively painting a picture on a canvas, left-handed. I got up and felt urgently that I had to tell him about the dream before July 4th: Independence Day, for whatever reason. I didn't know his number, so again I waited. I could have called the operator for the number of the White House, but I didn't. I marched through the woods in my backyard spouting my speech to the imaginary.

I came back home and went back into my dreamtime, completely forgetting about the competition. Again, there was a stage set up for my public address. I told the world-audience what I saw. Years down the road, "President Kennedy called me up." I was stupidly shot, and the alligator fell from the sky in an apocalyptic shower. The dream continued and I became aware of something on me.

I took my left dream-hand and reached back to my right shoulder blade. There, lurking, was the densest mess of symbols I have ever encountered. I peeled them off considerably and all of them, clumped into a dark bundle, animating into a living scorpion—a black scorpion. Taking the tail in my right hand, out of the "fade to black" before me, came my love in the form of a female lion. She approached and took the scorpion sting on her left cheek. She fell back and turned into a woman . . . dead.

Immediately, beneath my feet an abyss opened. I looked down and intuitively dropped the venom-less scorpion into it. Behind me appeared a white-winged messenger with a Bible open. The book's pages were fanning towards the end. The angel was being held back by a Great Wind as I faced south by southwest. When the last pages were reached, he stopped the unfurl. My mind got in the way for a moment, but he promptly tore them out. The abyss was still open at my feet. I looked down again cautiously but a brown, great-maned Lion arose from out of the chasm. He stepped forward, bent down and licked the left breast of my woman like a cat offered a bowl of milk. In gesture of penance, He smiled at me, cleaned both sides of his cheeks with that sense of satisfaction, and turned, bounding to go back to sleep within central Africa.

I glanced back but before the Lion comfortably nodded off, he motioned to affirm the way the angel had left the end of his book . . . unwritten.

I looked at the feminine form at my feet. Her nipples began to divide so fast, they inverted, became as numerous as alveoli and she took a breathe of life again.

With that, I started to come out of the trance. I looked left, and there were dolphins lined at the surface of the ocean. When my eyes met the "dolphins," they plunged into the water to mend the continental divide like needle and thread. A picture of The Little Mermaid flashed in full color, front and center. When I went to look for Ursula, my righteous rock-climbing friend, who had built the abridged two towers for the competition, I was physically absent from, rang my cell phone, and I "woke" up.

# 55

I didn't answer. How could I? I called back later and my friend's answering machine message, recorded by his wife, told me that I had stepped out of time.

To say I believe or interpret this dream fully is to just admit insanity. I understand the balance of things. This is just what the Seventh White Seal now looks like to me if given depth, counter and clockwise motion:

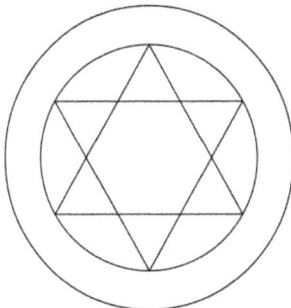

The Bible says that the Heavens went silent for thirty minutes when the Seventh Seal was/is opened (Revelation 8:1, NIV). That is all it says. The White Seal is a story from the Jungle Books by Rudyard Kipling.

Before I moved to Cascade, Idaho from Pocatello, I had been playing music with a friend of mine named David. As I was uprooting from that city in April 2013, I had another dream about a bar in Boise, Idaho called the Neurolux. It had always been the venue I wished to play music at, but never have. In this dream, I stepped into the Neurolux venue and David was playing on the stage. It surprised me to see him up there like a solo Modest Mouse. I felt overjoyed and the dream faded away...That is also why I dare to say that I have seen the "star" of David.

# *56*

## 70TH OF 70-7'S

I can't remember exactly where I learned this from, bedsides reading the many books and logic—either from "Four Blood Moons" by John Hagee, "What Does *the* Future Hold" by C. Marvin Pate or just by talking with my father, Larry Glen Pottenger.

Seventieth of seventy-sevens is a type of time span. Each cycle is a measurement of seven years. This seven-year cycle is to go on for seventy cycles. Seventieth of Seventy-Sevens is the last seven years foretold in Biblical tribulation. After a very specific set of prophecies are fulfilled the countdown of seven years begins. Very near the end of those seven years there is an army amassed on the mountain of Armageddon overlooking Israel (the chosen city). Out of the clouds descends Jesus with his raptured few to destroy the entire Earth with fire except for the Select who have been faithful to the name of. He rebuilds the Earth and gives a perfect union back to the people. We all live happily ever after.

---

But the actual bible story doesn't go like that. The prophecies are confused by a "near-far" complex. Technically speaking, the "antichrist" may have already come. He may have already been in the form of Rome to destroy the temple that existed when Lesou was alive. After Jesus was traded for the rebel leader, Barnabus, he was killed on a cross. The Jewish rebellion, that was festering within the hearts of the Israelites, started to gain more momentum. The Roman ruler gathered an army and invaded Israel. The Roman leader declared himself God with his eagle staff in hand as the whole city was burning. There were more crucifixions in Israel than ever before and the streets ran red with blood. This "near-far" quality of the prophesy says that the world should have either seen the Second Coming of Christ within a seven-year radius of that event (near) or sometime in an unseen future repeated (far). 70 x 7 = 490 years. This is why Lesous was supposed to return about five hundred years after his death the year zero A.D.

The near-far complex also opens another problem... incremental change. The Rapture belief of current believers is something that developed much later in Church history. Vengeance has already been won through the Catholic Church over the Romans. Israel is liberated and due to that happening, the face of the enemy changed. The new enemy is Islam. Therefore, another antichrist must declare himself God within a third temple in order for the mainstream prophesy to be true.

This "unseen (far) future" requires a Jewish temple to be built atop the "mountain", where currently, the Islamic Dome on the Rock stands.

Some of the mainstream prophesies may or may not have already come to pass but that one thing remains unchanged for them: In order for any of this to take place in the way written there has to be a Jewish temple built atop of the ruins of the Dome on the Rock. So, the only real thing standing between the Biblical Day of the Second Coming/Age of Messiah is Daniel 9:20-27. It is written that Israel will "confirm a covenant" after rebuilding their temple. The Orthodox Jew doesn't care much for Lesou and still bears the sacrifice of animals to YHWH. Within the temple is where they intend to bring that practice back to life.

If a third temple in Israel is rebuilt the efforts of the Messiah would be null and a new Arabian Knight's war is a guarantee. By keeping the Dome on the Rock where it stands, is to me, the only honorable treaty of peace possible. If Islam was to come together and want Israel to have the Temple Mount back then there may lie a "new covenant".

Who really knows what the covenant may be, but without Islam "happy" about the destruction of their Dome on the Rock, it is very unknown.

"Them be fighting words if I ever heard!"

I don't want to see the Jewish nation become another Emperor of Japan. Please, understand how eerie it is for me when I compare Atomic *Genbaku* Dome of Hiroshima,

Japan and the Dome on the Rock of Islam in Israel...
Destroying the Dome must rebuild it and rebuild it.

# 57

After the seven years of Revelation are over, the souls of the antichrist and the beast *are/were* imprisoned but for only one-thousand years. There is yet again another judgement. Satan is let out of the fiery core to test the people all over again (Revelation 20-22). For how long will this test last? All the same, it is *after* the one-thousand and seven years are over, is when the Earth is said to be destroyed by fire and the old order of things falls away . . . So, because the Earth hasn't been destroyed and the cycle of birth and death (the old order of things) hasn't been done away with, means either that the one-thousand years isn't over, the test isn't over or has yet to begin. The dilemma of the "near-far" complex is, if the "antichrist" has already been and isn't intended to come again, then the events of Revelation are entirely antiquated. Daniel of the Old Testament was the Dreamer of the temple defiler (aka the Roman conqueror/

antichrist). John was the dreamer of the book of Revelation in the New Testament. The fact that John was *in* prison and one of the only survivors of the Roman invasion, it isn't surprising that he started having dreams of revenge.

Please also note, that after the Second Coming of Christ, the Earth is still just the Earth, for the entire duration of the one thousand years. On this same Earth we live on, is where the Messiah rules. Biblically, even after the new Heaven and Earth are built, there are dogs and evil doers outside of the golden city (Rev. 22:15).

I can't stress this point enough. Revelation was never meant to get into the hands of triumphalism. Chaos has thrived through it for too long to not have learned from its double-edged karma. YHWH spells out the ending and gives us an opportunity to divert it (just like with Noah.) Looking at this again, it seems that I'm making the prediction that in 3020 A.D. the Earth is destroyed by fire, but I can't think that on my own.

I am Mowgli. I looked for my animal friends after leaving the Jungle. I couldn't find them in the form of the panther or bear. Kaa...the great snake was never the enemy if one reads up on it. If enemies change forms so rapidly, then what are we really dealing with?

## MY FORMULA IS:

Keep mending the brotherhood through falconry, love the Dome where it is, lead by example, learn the language and accept that no matter what, the Earth was meant to last for another thousand years past any End Time revelation/horror story. If the whales and the frogs die out, I don't see much reason for having faith in humanity anymore.

# 58

"GIVE US THIS DAY,

OUR DAILY BREAD,"

UNLESS YOU'RE ALLERGIC TO GLUTEN.

How could anyone say, "God the Creator" without immediately looking around and imply, "the God of Creativity?" What difference does it make whether it is four-thousand years old or a billion? For musicians, time is not a constant. It is sped up and slowed down every day; traced and retraced, then traced again in order to learn something either forgotten or previously unknown.

Carbon based life is not something to be called linear. If someone flatlines it is imminent death. The youth avoids a permanent emotional state and breeds an environment that won't just discord and die, due to microscopic dissonances in the sine wave of matter=paradox. We are then confronted with the littered portals daily, to the same universe where the "meanings" may be both created and destroyed. Meet Shiva, the Dismantler: The Black Hole of Post-Modernism…

*59*

## Cosmological Revolver
### *Allah listens when a little frog laughs*

Father of Heavens
Lesou
Holy Spirit-that-moves-in-All-things

*Isaac= He laughs*

Self-critiqued
Teachers
The Hunt

*Ishmael= Allah listens*

Mother of Havens
Those-that-play-well-together
Ecstatic Dance

*Mowgli= Little Frog*

# *Book References*

*Tales of Old Japan*, A. B. Mitford (Lord Redesdale)

*The Doors of Perception and Heaven and Hell*, Aldous Huxley

*The Count of Monte Cristo*, Alexandre Dumas

*Webster's Ninth New Collegiate Dictionary*, A Merriam Webster

*Bhagivad Gita: Krishna's Counsel in Time of War*, Translated by Barbara Stoler Miller

*Economic Botany 3rd edition: Plants in our world*, Beryl Brintnall Simpson and Molly Conner Ogorzaly

*The Fire from Within*, Carlos Castenada

*Swindoll's New Testament Insights, Insights on Luke*, Charles R. Swindoll

*Bulfinch's Mythology, Modern Abridgement*, Edmund Fuller

*Desert Solitaire: A Season in the Wilderness*, Edward Abbey

*Cosmology: The Science of the Universe 2nd edition*, Edward Harrison

*The Gyrfalcon*, Eugen Potapov and Richard Sale

*Dune*, Frank Herbert

*A Falconry Manuel*, Frank L. Beebe

*Beyond Good and Evil*, Frederich Nietszche

*Tao of Physics*, Fritjof Capra

*Tibetan Book of the Dead: First Complete Translation*, Translated by Gyurme Dorje

*Walden*, Henry David Thoreau

*Moby Dick*, Herman Melville

*The Zondervan Parallel New Testament in Greek and English,* Holy Bible

*Dharma Bums,* Jack Kerouac

*Guns, Germs, and Steel: The Fate of Human Societies,* Jared Diamond

*Catcher in the Rye*, J.D Salinger

*The Cosmic Serpent,* Jeremy Narby

*No One Here Gets Out Alive: The Biography of Jim Morrison,* Jerry Hopkins and Danny Sugerman

*What Does the Future Hold*, C. Marvin Pate

*Wolf Totem*, Jiang Rong

*CranioSacral Therapy,* John E. Upledger

*Outdoor Survival Skills*, Larry Dean Olsen

*Japan, Lonely Planet*

*The Multi-Orgasmic Man*, Mantak Chia and Douglas Abrams Arava

*The Lost World Jurassic Park*, Micheal Crichton

*Imprint Accipiter II,* Micheal McDermott

*The End of America,* Naomi Wolf

*Zen Flesh Zen Bones,* Compiled by Paul Reps and Nyogen Senzaki

*Reptiles and Amphibians: Eastern/Central North America*, Peterson's Field Guides

*The Magical and Ritual Use of Aphrodisiacs*, Richard Alan Miller

*Voices of the First Day: Awakening in the Aboriginal Dreamtime,* Robert Lawlor

*The Jungle Books*, Rudyard Kipling

*The Poetry of Zen,* Translated by Sam Hamill and J.P. Seaton

*New Concise Japanese- English Dictionary,* Sanseido

*Eagle Dreams: Searching for Legends in Wild Mongolia*, Stephen J. Bodio

*Hammer of the Gods,* Stephen Davis

*The Way of Chuang Tzu,* Thomas Merton

*Electric Kool-Aid Acid Test*, Tom Wolfe

# Music References

*I Shall Be Free*, Bob Dylan

*Running Through The Jungle*, Creedence Clearwater Revival

*Find the Cost of Freedom,* Crosby, Stills, Nash and Young

*Not To Touch The Earth*, The Doors

*Rikki-Tikki-Tavi,* Donovan

*Barlyk,* Huun-Huur-tu

*Voodoo Chile*, The Jimi Hendrix Experience

*Jurassic Park Theme Song*, John Williams

*21st Century Schizoid Man*, King Crimson

*Good News For People Who Love Bad News*, Modest Mouse

*Love's Not Dead*, The Mowgli's

*Lithium,* Nirvana

*Roxanne,* The Police

*The Pride of Man,* Quicksiver Messenger Service

*The Pusher,* Steppenwolf

*Lateralus*, Undertow, Ænima, Tool

*Pomps and Prides,* Toots and The Maytals

*Excess,* Tricky

# Movie References

*Fight Club,* David Fincher
*Star Wars,* Gorge Lucas
*Jurassic Park*, Steven Spielberg
*The Jungle Book*, Walt Disney
*The Lion King,* Walt Disney
*The Little Mermaid*, Walt Disney

# Website References

http://nhkox.homestead.com/who1.htmlwikipedia.org

# About the Author

**Isaac** first published *Mowgli's Almanac* in April of 2014. The book got rewritten over the next six years, on and off, while working falconry-based bird abatement. He built his own tiny A-frame in the mountains of Idaho and continued his travels in Japan. He has taught yoga and English and worked as a Thai massage therapist. Isaac was aired on *Animal Planet's*, "Rugged Justice" TV show in the falconer episode of 2015. Residing with his pack of dogs and sanctuary of birds, his next sojourn begins.